End Times Scripture Handbook For

Powerful, Strategic Praying

2nd Edition

Compiled by
Cheryl Zehr

Olive Press
צהר זית
Messianic & Christian Publisher
Rochester, NY 14609 and
Port Leyden, NY 13433

End Times Scripture Handbook For Powerful, Strategic Praying

Copyright © 1st Edition 2006 and 2007 by Cheryl Zehr
Copyright © 2nd Edition 2009 by Cheryl Zehr
All rights reserved

ISBN 978-0-9790873-0-1

Published by
    Olive Press צהר זית
Messianic and Christian Publisher
P. O. Box 567
Port Leyden, NY 13433
www.olivepresspublisher.org

Our prayer at Olive Press is that we may help make the Word of Adonai fully known, ... and spread rapidly and be glorified everywhere. May our books help open people's eyes so they will turn from darkness to Light and from the power of the adversary to God and ... trust in ישוע Yeshua (Jesus).
(From II Thess. 3:1; Col. 1:25; Acts 26:18,15 NRSV and CJB, the Complete Jewish Bible)
    May this book in particular inspire people to become intercessors for the above things for the world.

They overcame
…by the Blood of the Lamb
and by the Word…
Rev. 12:11

"Word" here in Greek is "Logos." It is the same word used in John 1:1. *And the Word was with God. And the Word was God.* This handbook is to help people do powerful, strategic praying with the Word of God. The Word is mighty and powerful, and accomplishes the purpose for which God sends it. When we pray Scriptures, we are praying the *power* of God Himself. And we *will* overcome!

Forward

In Ephesians 6 Rabbi Sha'ul (Apostle Paul) tells us that to be able to stand in Spiritual Warfare we need to take up the Word of God and use it to pray at all times, in the Spirit, vigilantly, persistently for all God's people. *And take ... the sword given by the Spirit, that is, the Word of God; as you pray at all times, with all kinds of prayers and requests, in the Spirit, vigilantly and persistently, for all God's people* (Ephesians 6:17-18) (Complete Jewish Bible, David H. Stern, Jewish New Testament Publications, Inc. 1998). Sha'ul is telling us that we need to know what the Word says about a given subject and pray that Word for that subject. Then we will be able to stand against the powers of darkness.

Yeshua also tells us in John 15:7 that it is His words abiding in us that causes our prayers to be effective. *"If you remain united with me, and my words with you, then ask whatever you want, and it will happen for you."* He means that when we know His words regarding a subject of prayer and pray according to them, we will be praying God's will for that situation, and thus, our prayers will be answered, that is they will be effective. However, few believers are capable of praying the Words of God for the many diverse subjects the Ruakh (Holy Spirit) leads us to pray for, because few are familiar enough with the Bible to know what God has said about the many areas that are in need of prayer. It would take a very accomplished Bible scholar and memorizer to be able to remember Bible passages relating to the many topics for which the Ruakh calls us to pray. How can we hope to be effective in our praying when, out of ignorance, we are incapable of using the mighty Sword the Lord has given us?

In *Powerful, Strategic Praying* Cheryl Zehr provides a strategic tool to make our intercession more effective by increasing our ability to wield the Word. She gives us a resource to enhance our use of the Scriptures as the Sword of the Spirit. This book contains compilations of Scriptures that can be prayed for various important subjects. It enables the application of the Word to the subjects for which we are praying, thus fulfilling both Rabbi Sha'ul and Yeshua's instruction to us.

Cheryl has created a comprehensive list of prayer topics that cover most of the areas for which the Ruakh leads us to pray in these end times, and has compiled a comprehensive collection of Scriptures concerning each topic. We simply need to refer to her table of contents to find the subject for which we are praying and begin to pray those Scriptures. Cheryl has also recorded, from her personal journal, anointed prayers she has prayed over the years on each of these subjects to help us intercede for these areas. Cheryl is an excellent writer and manages to communicate her passion in writing down her prayers on each subject.

This book is a very valuable contribution to the true intercessors of the Kingdom of God from a true intercessor.

Rabbi Jim Appel
Rochester, NY

I dedicate this book to
**Yeshua Adonai,
Jesus, our Lord and Savior,**

from whom all things proceed, to whom all things belong,
and in whom all things hold together,

and to my husband, Glenn,
who is giving his life and his all as a living sacrifice to the Lord.
I esteem him highly and love him deeply for it.

Contents

Technical Notes

Bible Translations:

I chose the New Revised Standard Version as the main translation for this book because, to me, its wording is almost as poetically beautiful as the King James, yet it's meaning is very clear. And since it is not widely known it will give you a fresh look at some of the more familiar Scriptures.

NRSV- New Revised Standard Version
NKJV- New King James Version
NIV- New International Version
KJV- King James Version
AMP- Amplified Bible
note- an NRSV footnote giving an alternate Hebrew meaning of a word

Capitalization:

I grew up with a King James Bible which honored God by capitalizing all pronouns that refer to God, Jesus, or the Holy Spirit. I like honoring God this way, so I have capitalized them even if the versions I'm using don't. I also capitalized "name" when it refers to the Name of Jesus, and I capitalized "word" when it refers to the Word or Words of God, because Jesus "was the Word and the Word was with God and the Word was God." Anything that is referring to any part of the Trinity, I like to capitalize out of reverence. I also like to capitalize words like "Glory," "Life," and "Light," etc. when they refer to God. I don't give satan the honor of capitalizing his name.

Fonts and Line Spacing:

The Scriptures are all in this Arial Narrow font *or in italics.* Whenever it is just me talking it is in this plain Times New Roman font. In the sections without headings, I grouped Scriptures together that are on the same topic. I put a space between the ones that are on a slightly different subject. Sometimes I put a space just to make the Scripture stand out more.

Skipping parts of verses:

I put down only parts of some verses for two reasons. The first one is because I want you to see it in a different light. Sometimes we know a passage so well that we actually miss what is in it. To give the phrase a greater impacting punch, I sometimes even break a grammatical rule by not putting an ellipse (...) at the end (or at the beginning when I left off a small word like "and" or "for"). I hope you will forgive me. The second reason is because those are the parts of the verses that fit in those categories. You, of course, are free to check out the full passages yourself.

These lists of Scriptures are by no means exhaustive. I even left out some well-known Scriptures. There is space in the margins and at the end of most of the sections for you to add Scriptures.

Being Ready for Powerful, Strategic Praying

A person doing spiritual warfare praying needs to be free from the entanglement of evil and from all demonic influences. Please spend time searching your heart before the Lord before you begin. In his book *Watchman on the Wall – A Practical Guide to Prayer for Jerusalem and Her People* (Kairos Publishing, Clarence, NY, 2005), Robert Stearns has a section called "A Spiritual Checklist for Effective Intercession." I strongly recommend you go through that, or something similar, and I also **most urgently advise** you to attend a special spiritual house-cleaning retreat like *The Cleansing Stream Seminar* (www.cleansingstream.org) before stepping into this handbook. (My husband and I went through it in May 2005. We were amazed at how light and free we felt and how much bolder we became for Jesus.)

You who remind the Lord, take no rest, and give Him no rest. Isaiah 62:7

PRELIMINARY PREPARATIONS

RECEIVE YOUR ORDERS:

The Scriptural Mandate
to Pray for Prophecies
to Come to Pass

This handbook is intended for serious Believers who have an intimate relationship with Jesus (Yeshua) and a solid foundation in the Word of God, who have an urgent sense that the end of the age is near, who are spending much time crying out in prayer for the world and Israel, and who are begging for Jesus to return. Or it is for anyone who wants to become one of those kinds of Believers. Did I describe you? Then welcome.

This book came out of my time in the secret place with the Lord Jesus. In 1997 God arranged my circumstances and called me to be a "Mary" full time—to sit at Jesus' feet, all day, to listen to Him, to soak in His Word, to ponder and meditate on it. (For this I will never be able to thank Jesus enough.)

At first, my time at His feet was mostly a season of Him exposing my blackness, and me repenting in tears of Godly sorrow, and being cleansed by His blood. Then it was a few years of Him transforming my thinking with His Word. (Again, I will never be done thanking Him, not even in eternity.) Finally I graduated to doing intercessory prayer for people.

Then in 2004, I read an article in the March/April issue of *Pray! Magazine*, by Steve Hawthorne about praying for the nations. It tugged my heart. I wrote in my journal, "*I* want to pray for nations to worship Jesus! It excites me!! It is like Daniel praying for his nation to be delivered from Babylon when he read the prophesy in Jeremiah. We have the prophecy in Revelation that *a multitude that no man can count from every tribe, tongue, nation, and people* will be praising God. We need to pray like Daniel for that prophesy to be fulfilled!! Surely the time is here!" In an insert in the magazine, Cynthia Bezek listed some Psalms about nations coming to the Lord. I searched in Psalms for more but found only a few.

My cry for the nations became a cry for the world to be delivered from the evil one, for God's Kingdom to come and His will to be done "on earth as it is in heaven." The more I prayed, the more increasingly terrible things kept happening in the world—the Iraq war got worse, the Tsunami happened, etc—until it became apparent to me that we must be getting right on the edge of the end times.

On September 17, 2005 I asked Jesus to show me how to pray the exact, strategic prayers needed. I expected to be given "groanings that cannot be uttered." But God answered in a different way. The very next day, my pastor, Jack Hempfling, used the Scripture, I Timothy 1:18 *This charge I give you...according to the prophecies previously made concerning you, that by them you may **wage a good warfare*** (NKJV). He pointed out that when we get prophecies over us we should use them in prayer warfare to pray that they come to pass. This reinforced what I had learned from my intercessory prayer leader, Jim Eby, and what I knew of the power of praying the Word, but I hadn't yet thought of it as spiritual warfare.

On September 28 I visited a Elim Bible Institute class and Professor Sylvia Evans, an anointed woman of God, spoke on Jeremiah 23:22. *But if they had stood in My council, then they would have proclaimed My Words to My people and they would have turned them from their evil way and from the evil of their doings.*

I was deeply touched by that Scripture. The next day I read the whole chapter. Verses 19 and 20 shocked me—having just seen hurricanes Katrina, Wilma, and Rita in the news! *Look, the storm of the Lord! Wrath has gone forth, a whirling tempest [KJV: a grievous whirlwind]; it will burst upon the head of the wicked. The anger of the Lord will **not turn back until** He has executed and accomplished the intents of His mind. **In the latter days you will understand it clearly.*** The last sentence really startled me.

I began to understand one thing clearly—that I was supposed to use end time prophecies as warfare to do serious praying that they actually come to pass! I began right away with the few verses I had.

On October 19, 2005 the Holy Spirit guided me to more Scriptures declaring that nations will turn to the Lord. I typed them all up on the computer. Then I walked around my prayer room, reading them and doing prayer warfare with them.

After that, end time Scriptures came to me in floods. Wherever I felt led to read for my quiet times, there I would find more. In November, I took the now growing list with me on a short-term mission trip to El Salvador to do spiritual warfare there. Then on November 30, my sister loaned me Beth Moore's book, *Praying God's Word* (Broadman and Coleman, Nashville, TN, 2000). The chapter, "Overcoming the Enemy," gave me the idea of putting together a list of spiritual warfare Scriptures to read over and over to strengthen me for my prayer battling. In 2005, I took my lists with me on a short trip to Israel and used them to pray over Jerusalem. I had no idea all this would become a book. I thank God for that with all my heart. In October 2006 I took a pre published print-out of this book with me when I moved to Jerusalem for a school year.

[Some of the lists in here are actually from years back. The "Word of God" section, for example, started as a poster I made and put on the wall over the dinner table for my children and I. They were Scriptures that my pastor father had taught me as a child. The poster-over-the-dinner-table idea came from my mother. (I am so grateful to my parents for raising me in the Word.)]

I hope you will find this book to be a very useful tool. Some of these lists can be used for prayers for your personal life. For example, the "Spiritual Warfare" section could be used for any attack from the enemy anywhere, and the "World's Wisdom" one could be used to pray against the foolishness in your wayward teen's mind. But that is not the main purpose of this book. This book is geared for global praying. It is to be used by world intercessory prayer warriors—the Daniel's, Nehemiah's, Anna's and Simeon's of today.

Are you called by God to be one of them? If you are, then let's join together in using the mighty, unshakable, earth-shattering, life-changing Word of God to do powerful, strategic praying for the world in these end times. Let's remind the Lord of His Word and give Him no rest.

This charge I give you...according to the prophecies previously made concerning you, that by them you may *wage* a *good warfare*. I Tim 1:18 NKJV

You who remind the Lord, take no rest, and give Him no rest until He establishes Jerusalem and makes it renown throughout the earth. Is. 62:7

Let's take the Bible verses about the mighty, foretold works of God that have not yet come to pass, and use them to pray fighting, believing prayers that call them into existence and fulfillment like Daniel did.

I, Daniel, understood from the Scriptures, according to the Word of the Lord given to Jeremiah, the prophet, that the desolation of Jerusalem would last seventy years. So I turned to the Lord God and pleaded with Him in prayer and petition, in fasting, and in sackcloth and ashes. Dan. 9:2-3 NIV

O Lord, Listen and act and do not delay! Dan. 9:19

And like Nehemiah did.

O Lord God of heaven, the great and awesome God who keeps covenant and steadfast love with those who love Him and keep His commandments; Let Your ear be attentive and Your eyes open to hear the prayer of Your servant that I now pray before You day and night... **Remember the Word that You commanded**.... Neh. 1:8,9

Daniel goes on to repent for his people's sins and to affirm that their punishment was a fulfillment of God's Word. Then he pleads for the captivity to end as Jeremiah had prophesied it would. He works hard in prayer for a prophecy to be fulfilled. This is what we want to do for end time prophecies. And like Daniel, we must also start our warfare praying with full repentance and confession of sin before the Lord, for ourselves first and then for our families and our nations. The sections on God's judgment will help us do that. When we see how fierce God's judgment can be, it brings us to our knees.

...I was speaking and praying and confessing my sin and the sin of my people Israel, and presenting my supplication before the Lord my God on behalf of the holy mountain of my God.... Dan. 9:20

Nehemiah and Ezra are other examples of this.

...Confessing the sins of the people of Israel, which we sinned against you. Both I and my family have sinned. We have offended you deeply.... Neh. 1:6-7

"O my God, I am too ashamed and embarrassed to lift my face to You, my God, for our iniquities have risen higher than our head, and our guilt has mounted up to the heavens." Ezra 9:6

As we remind the Lord in our prayer warfare, let's expect great things to happen!

The one who believes in Me...will do greater works than these... Jn. 14:12

The people who are loyal to their God shall stand firm and take action. Dan. 11;32

The people who know their God shall be strong and shall carry out great exploits.
Dan. 11:32 NKJV

The Father...will show him greater works than these, so that you will be astonished.
Jn. 5:20

Look at the nations, and see! Be astonished! Be astounded! For a work is being done in your days that you would not believe if you were told. Hab. 1:5

I stand in awe, O Lord, of Your work. In our own time revive it. In our own time make it known. Hab. 3:1

Reading on in Daniel 10, we can see that it's possible his praying and fasting may have helped the angels in their battle against the "prince of Persia." May our praying and fasting today have such profound affects in the heavenlies. In fact, let's trust God for even greater impact. Let's pray and battle together with Jesus and His angelic hosts to banish satan and all his evil hordes from the earth completely! (See Rev. 20:10 and pp. 175-179 in this book.)

The greatest works are that people turn to the Lord:

I did not send the prophets yet they ran; I did not speak to them yet they prophesied. But if they had stood in My council, then they would have proclaimed My Words to My people and they would have turned them from their evil way and from the evil of their doings. Jer. 23:21-22

And that the Lord be glorified:

We do not make requests of You because we are righteous, but because of Your great mercy. O Lord, listen! O Lord, forgive! O Lord, hear and act! For Your sake, O my God, do not delay, because Your city and Your people bear Your Name. Dan. 9:18-19 NIV (Today it is not only Israel that bears God's Name. The whole world sees America as a Christian nation and President Bush as a Christian man. Even in the remote desert of Mongolia where I went, they do.)

Let's stand now in God's council and pray His Word, so that *His* astounding works will be done.

Suggestions For How To Use This Book

In Private:

You may use this book in your private devotion time to stir your faith and to inspire you to pray. First prepare your heart with the first eight preliminary sections. Take as many days or weeks as you need to do that. Go over those sections repeatedly, reading them out loud, pausing to meditate phrase by phrase, until the Truths in those Scriptures renew your mind and become part of you. With the Holy Spirit's anointing, the Word of God will have profound, belief-changing affect on your thinking, giving you the courage and strong faith you need to pray earth-shattering prayers.

Then move on to the lists of prophetic Scriptures, seeking God each time as to which section He wants you to focus on. Read the list aloud to stir up the Spirit of intercession within you. Then ask the Holy Spirit to help you turn the Scriptures one at a time into prayers. In this way you will be doing serious, strategic praying that will move heaven to change things on earth. Record your prayers in this book or in your journal so you don't miss God's awesome answers. Be sure to end with worship, using, for example, the last section in this book.

In Groups:

In intercessory prayer meetings, with the Holy Spirit's leading, choose one or two of the first eight preliminary sections to read out loud in a meditative way to build the group's faith. Then seek God's direction for which section to focus on for your strategic, end time praying. Your leader/moderator can read one verse or phrase out loud, and then let the group pray awhile using that verse. Then the leader can read another phrase, and let the group do more praying. Continue in this manner until the end, interspersing your prayers with songs as the Holy Spirit leads. End with one of the worship sections. Keep track of what your group prays for. You will be amazed at how God answers!!

Using the Prayers in this Book:

I often write my prayers to Jesus. As I write them I sometimes have the sense that I am praying exactly what the Lord wants me to pray. I feel His power flowing through me onto the page. I sense the same anointing as I pray them out loud over and over in the following days. Through the years God has answered many of my written prayers.

I have included some of my (edited) journal prayers in this book to inspire you to pray. Please go ahead and pray them as if they were your own words, if you'd like, until your own creative prayers well up within you. There is space at the end of most of the sections for you to write your prayers. May the Holy Spirit's anointing fill you as you pray.

Prayer About the Mandate

Sept.17, '05

O Jesus, You know what is going on in the heavenlies!! You know the exact, strategic prayers I need to be praying. Help me to pray those powerful, strategic prayers in the Holy Spirit.

Jan. 9, '06

Jesus, thank You for all the people who have been strong and have carried out great exploits for You. I want to be one of them, Jesus. Purify me and make me ready. I want to carry out Your great work. I want to help lead thousands and millions to You.

The...fervent prayer of a righteous man avails much. James 5:16 _{NKJV}

PURIFY YOURSELF:

Things That Hinder
Our Prayers

Let's use this Words from God to examine our lives and repent (Prov. 28:9) before God in peparation for spiritual warfare.

Not praying His Will:
Matt. 6: 9,10 "Pray then in this way: …**Your will be done**, on earth as it is in heaven."

Asking for our own will instead of God's Will:
James 4:3 You ask and do not receive, because you ask wrongly, in order to spend what you get on your pleasures.

Living in Disagreement (God loves unity and agreement):
Matt. 18:18 "If two of you **agree** on earth about anything you ask, it will be done for you by My Father."
I Pet. 3:7 Husbands, in the same way, show consideration for your wives in your life together, paying honor to the woman…so that **nothing may hinder your prayers**.
Titus 2:3 Encourage the young women to love their husbands, to love their children, to be self-controlled, chaste, good managers of the household, being submissive to their husbands, so that the **Word of God may not be discredited** [NKJV: **blasphemed**].
Matt. 5:23-24 "So when you are offering your gift at the altar, if you remember that your brother [or sister] has something against you, leave your gift; …**first be reconciled to your brother** [or sister]."

Unbelief:
James 1:7-8 …for the **doubter**, being double-minded and unstable in every way, must not expect to receive anything from the Lord.
Matt. 13: 58 And He **did not** do many deeds of power there, because of their **unbelief.**
Mk. 6:5-6 And He could do **no deed of power** there, except that He laid His hands on a few sick people and cured them. And He was amazed at their **unbelief.**
Mk. 9:24 Immediately the father of the child **cried out**, "I **believe**; Help my **unbelief!**" (Jesus helped his unbelief. He healed his boy.)
Mk. 16:14 …and He upbraided them for their **lack of faith** and stubbornness, because they had **not believed**….
Lk. 24:25 Jesus said, "O how foolish you are, and how **slow of heart to believe** all that the prophets have declared!"
Mk. 16:17 And these signs will accompany those who **believe**….

Complaining:
Numbers 11:1 Now when the people **complained** in the hearing of the Lord about their misfortunes, the Lord heard it and His anger was kindled. Then the fire of the Lord burned against them.
Numbers 14:27-28 I have heard the **complaints** of the Israelites, which they **complain** against Me. Say to them, "As I live," says the Lord, "I will do to you the very things I heard you say."
The opposite of complaining is **thanksgiving**:
Ps. 69:30-31 I will magnify Him with **thanksgiving**. This will **please the Lord** more than an ox or a bull. (An ox or bull were the biggest sacrifices possible so giving thanks pleases the Lord more than just about anything!!!)
Ps. 51:23 Those who bring **thanksgiving** as their sacrifice **honor Me**.

Disobedience:

Prov. 1:25 Because you have **ignored all My counsel** and...My reproof, I will also laugh at your calamity...when panic strikes you.... [You] will call upon Me but I will not answer.

Prov. 28: 9 When one will **not listen to the Law**, *even one's prayers are an abomination.*

Prov. 15:8,29 The prayer of the **upright** is His delight. He hears the prayer of the **righteous**.

Nehemiah 1: 5 O Lord God of heaven, the great and awesome God who keeps covenant and steadfast love with those who love Him and **keep His commandments**...

Not being serious and disciplined:

I Pet. 4:7 ...be **serious** and **discipline** yourselves for the sake of your **prayers**.

Unforgiveness:

Mk. 11:25 "Whenever you stand praying, **forgive**, if you have *anything* against anyone."

Matt. 6:15 "But if you do not **forgive** others, neither will our Father **forgive** you...." (He's talking about praying here.)

Matt. 18:34-35 "His lord handed him over to be tortured.... So My heavenly Father will also do to every one of you, if you do not **forgive** your brother [or sister] from your heart."

(If God is handing us over to be tortured, I don't think He is going to be answering our prayers.)

Pride and rebellion:

Jn. 5:44 "How can you **believe** when **you accept glory** from one another...?"

Is. 63:10 But they **rebelled**...; therefore He [God] became their enemy. He Himself fought against them.

I Sam. 12:15 But if you...**rebel** against the...Lord...[His] hand...will be against you.

James 4:6 God resists the **proud**. (If the Lord is resisting us, He most likely won't be answering our prayers.)

Prov. 28: 9 When one will **not listen to the Law**, *even one's prayers are an abomination.*

Gossip and dishonesty:

Ps. 50:19 You sit and speak against your kin, ...You thought I was one just like yourself, but now I rebuke you.... I will tear you apart and there will be **no one to deliver**.

Ps. 5: 5 You [God] destroy those who speak **lies.**

Not being in reverent awe of God

Matt. 6:9 "Pray then in this way: Our Father in heaven, **hallowed** be Your Name."

Nehemiah 1:5 O Lord God of heaven, the **great and awesome God** who keeps covenant and steadfast love with those who love Him and keep His commandment. (God answered Nehemiah's prayer.)

Hidden Sin:

Ps. 66:18-19 If I had cherished **iniquity** in my heart, the Lord would **not have listened**. But truly God has listened; He has given heed to the words of my prayer.

Faith comes by hearing...the Word of God. Romans 10:17 nkjv

KNOW THE POWER AND AUTHORITY YOU ARE UNDER:

THE WORD OF GOD

One main weapon in our prayer battles is God's Word. Before using it we must have faith to believe that the **Word of God** is what God says it is! Here is a list of verses for us to read out loud (so we *hear* them) to increase our faith in the awesome, unshakeable, unchangeable, all powerful **Word of God**.

Jn. 1:1-2 In the beginning was the **Word** and the **Word** was with God, and the **Word** was God.... All things came into being through Him [the **Word**], and without Him not one thing came into being.

Gen. 1:3 And God said [His **Word**], "Let there be light and there was light."

Jn. 1:14 The **Word** became flesh and made His dwelling among us. We have seen His Glory, the Glory of the One and Only.

Heb. 4:12-13 Indeed the **Word** of God is living and active [KJV: quick and powerful], sharper than any two-edged sword...able to judge the thoughts and intentions of the heart... all [is] laid bare to the eyes of the One to whom we must render an account.

Is. 45:23 From My mouth has gone forth in righteousness a **Word** that shall not return.

Is. 31:2 He does not call back His **Words.**

Is. 55:11 So is the **Word** that goes out of My mouth; it will not return to Me empty, but will accomplish what I desire and achieve the purpose for which I sent it.

Jer. 1:12 Then the Lord said to me, "...I am watching over My **Word** to perform it."

Ps. 89:34 I will not violate My covenant, or alter the **Word** that went forth from My lips.

Micah 2:7 Do not My **Words** do good to one who walks upright?

Ps. 94:12 Blessed is the man You discipline, O Lord, the man You teach from Your **Law.** [The Law (or Torah) is the Word.].

Ps. 107:20 He sent out His **Word** and healed them and delivered them from destruction.

Lk 7:7 "But only speak the **Word**, and let my servant be healed." ...Jesus...was amazed at him.

Matt. 5:17 Jesus said, "Do not think that I have come to abolish the **law** or the **prophets** [the **Word**]; I have come...to **fulfill**. For truly I tell you, until heaven and earth pass away, not one letter, not one stroke of a letter, will pass from the **law** until all is accomplished."

Is. 40:8 The grass withers, the flower fades, but the **Word of God** stands forever.

Matt. 24:35 "Heaven and earth will pass away, but My **Words** shall not pass away."

I Pet. 1:25 The **Word of the Lord** endures forever. And this is the **Word** which is preached to you.

Ps. 119:89 Forever, O Lord, Your **Word** is settled in heaven (NKJV). Your **Word** is firmly fixed in heaven (NRSV).

Ps. 96:10 Your **Word** is firmly established. It shall never be moved.

Ps. 138:2b For You have exalted Your Name and Your **Word** above everything.

Lk. 24: 27 Then beginning with Moses and all the prophets, He interpreted to them...ALL the **Scriptures**.

Jn. 6:63 The **Words** that I have spoken to you are Spirit and Life.

Jn. 17:17 [Jesus prayed,] "Your **Word** is **Truth**."

Jn. 8:32 "And you shall know the **Truth,** and the **Truth** will set you free."

Ps. 119:160 The sum of Your **Word** is **Truth**.

Ps 119: 105 Your **Word** is...Light.

Jn. 15:23 "Those who love Me keep My **Word**."

Is. 66:2 This is the one to whom I will look, to the humble and contrite in spirit, who trembles at My **Word.**

Col. 3:17 Let the **Word of Christ** dwell in you richly.

Jn. 15: 7 "If you abide in Me and **My Word** abides in you, ask whatever you wish and it will be done for you."

Deut. 17:18-20 He [the king] shall have a copy of this **Law**.... It shall remain with him and he shall read in it all the days of his life, so that he may learn to fear the Lord his God, diligently observing all the **Words** of this **Law**...neither exalting himself...[nor] turning aside from the **commandment**, either to the right or to the left, so that he and his descendants may reign long. [The Law (or Torah) is the Word.]

Josh. 1:8 This **Book of Law** shall not depart out of your mouth; you shall meditate on it day and night, so that you may be careful to act in accordance with all that is written in it. For then you shall make your way prosperous, and then you shall be successful.

Prov. 13:13 Those who despise the **Word** bring destruction on themselves, but those who respect the commandment will be rewarded.

Ps. 1:2 But his delight is in the **Law of the Lord**, and on His **Law** he meditates day and night.... Whatever he does prospers. [The Law (or Torah) is the Word.]

Prov. 2:1-6,12 My child, if you accept My **Words** and treasure up My **commandments** within you...if you indeed cry out for insight, ...if you seek it like silver, and search for it as for hidden treasures—then you will understand.... For the Lord gives wisdom; from His mouth [His **Word**] come knowledge and understanding.... It will save you from the way of evil.

Prov. 4:20-22 My child, be attentive to My **Words**; incline your ear to My **sayings**. Do not let them escape from your sight; keep them within your heart, for they are life to those who find them, and healing to all their flesh [NIV: health to a man's whole body].

Ps. 119:11 I treasure Your **Word** in my heart that I might not sin against You.

Ps. 119:162 I rejoice at Your **Word**, like one who finds great spoil.

Ps. 119:130 The unfolding of your **Words** gives Light; it imparts understanding to the simple.

Ps. 119: 105 Your **Word** is a lamp to my feet and a light to my path.

2 Tim. 3:16 All **Scripture** [All of the **Word**] is inspired by God and is useful....

Rom. 10:17 Faith comes by hearing, and hearing by the **Word** of God (NKJV).
(Faith comes by hearing...the **Word** of God!)

Rev. 12:11 They overcame [the enemy] by the Blood of the Lamb and by the **Word** (KJV).

II Tim. 2:15 Do your best to present yourself to God as one who...correctly handles the **Word of Truth** (NIV).

Eph. 6:17 Take...the sword of the Spirit, which is the **Word** of God.

Jer. 23:21-22 But if they had stood in My council, then they would have proclaimed My **Words** to My people and they would have turned them from their evil way and from the evil of their doings.

Jer. 23:29 Let the one who has My **Word** speak My **Word** faithfully.... Is not My **Word** like fire, says the Lord, and like a hammer that breaks a rock in pieces?

Is. 44:24-25 I am the Lord, who...confirms the **Word** of His servant, and fulfills the prediction of His messengers.

Ps. 103:20 Bless the Lord, O you His angels, you mighty ones who do His bidding, obedient to His spoken **Word.**

Mk. 8:38 "Those who are ashamed of Me and of My **Words** in this adulterous and sinful generation, of them the Son of Man will also be ashamed...."

Ps. 119:161, 167 My heart stands in awe of Your **Words**.... I love them exceedingly.

Ps. 119:114,147 I hope in Your **Word**.... I put my hope in Your **Word**.

Heb. 1:3 He [Jesus] sustains all things by His Powerful **Word**.

(Add your own verses on the Word of God here.)

Prayer about the Word of God

O Yeshua Adonai, Your Word is so precious and so majestic. You sustain the whole world by Your powerful Word. All the earthly powers trying to destroy the world are no match against the might of Your Word! Help me to abide in Your almighty, everlasting Word.

Psalms 1 tells us to meditate on Your Word day and night. That doesn't leave any time for meditating on much else. So help me, Lord, not to meditate or ponder on anything else but Your Word—not on my own words or on other people's words whether in great books, in movies or in conversations—only on Your Word! Help me keep my thoughts full of Your WORD.

You said if Your Words abide in us You will give us whatever we ask (Jn. 15:7) so the power of prayer is not only in praying Your Word, but also in abiding in You and Your Word. O Yeshua HaMeshiach (the Messiah), help us to soak in Your word every day—to study it, memorize it, ponder on it, and obey it until Your Words become the core of our very being. Then we will see the full power of praying Your Word and Your Will.

(This book came into being when I was just starting to use Jesus' original Name, Yeshua, which means "salvation" in Hebrew. Therefore mostly in here you will see Jesus, His English Name, used. I believe there is power in His Name in every language! Although, to me, there is something extra special about hearing His Hebrew Name, especially in Israel.)

May 1, '00

When our teenage daughter came home from work last night, I said hi, but she didn't even look at me. She barely acknowledged me and went straight to the computer. When I asked what she was doing she said, "I gotta change something." She had been thinking about what she'd written in a saved e-mail all the way home, and that was much more important than her ole' mom.

That convicted me today. How many times have I been focused on my own words to the point of ignoring Jesus. We are supposed to meditate on His Word not on our own puny, insignificant words.

Thank you, Lord Jesus for this revelation. Help me to focus on You and Your Word.

June 20, '00

Thy Word have I hid in my heart that I might not sin against Thee (Ps. 119:11 KJV). It doesn't say, "...that I might look smart and wise to others" or "so I can see others faults and point them out to them." No, it is so I can see my OWN faults!! Help us, Jesus, to use Your Word to see our own faults so we can repent and be cleansed!!

June 29, '00

O that I could get to the place where I am like a tree planted by streams of water (The streams of water are God's Word!!) and to where everything I do prospers. But to get there I must be delighted in God's Word so much that I meditate on it day and night—not on other things!!!

Help me get to that meditating place, Jesus. I *am* getting there a little, aren't I, Lord? Someday I will by Your grace and mercy and by Your Blood.

(Write your own prayers about God's Word here and on the next page.)

They meditate day and night. Psalms 1:2

KNOW AND WORSHIP
YOUR COMMANDER:

Our Glorious Savior

To further prepare our minds and build our faith, let's meditate on Jesus. Read the Scriptures out loud first. Then meditate.

O Lord my God, You are very great.
You are clothed with honor and majesty,
Wrapped in Light as with a garment.
You stretch out the heavens like a tent,
You set the beams of Your chambers on the waters,
You make the clouds Your chariot,
You ride on the wings of the wind,
You make the winds Your messengers,
Fire and flame Your ministers. Ps. 104:1-4

Lift up a song to Him who rides upon the clouds....
O Rider in the heavens, the ancient heavens;
Listen, He sends out His voice, His mighty voice...
Whose power is in the skies.
Awesome is God in His sanctuary....
He gives power and strength to His people.
Blessed be God! Ps. 68:4,33-35

There is none like God...who rides through the heavens to your help,
majestic through the skies. Deut. 33:26

Glorious are You, more majestic than the everlasting mountains. Ps. 76:4

The voice of the Lord flashes forth flames of fire.
The voice of the Lord shakes the wilderness.
The voice of the Lord causes oaks to whirl and strips the forest bare.
And in His temple ALL say, "Glory!" Ps. 29:5-9

In the following verses I put Jesus' Name in place of "He, His, Him," etc. Read each phrase out loud first. Then meditate on it.

He [God] has rescued us from the power of darkness
And transferred us into the Kingdom of His beloved Son,
In whom we have redemption, the forgiveness of sins.
[Jesus] is the image of the invisible God, the firstborn of all creation;
For in **Jesus** all things in heaven and on earth were created,
Things visible and invisible, whether thrones or dominions or rulers or powers
—all things have been created through **[Jesus]** and for **[Jesus]**.
[Jesus] Himself is before all things,
And in **[Jesus]** all things hold together.
[Jesus] is the head of the body, the church;
[Jesus] is the beginning, the firstborn from the dead,
So that **[Jesus]** might come to have first place in everything.
For in **[Jesus]** all the fullness of God was pleased to dwell,
And through **[Jesus]** God was pleased to reconcile to Himself all things,

Whether on earth or in heaven, by making
Peace through the Blood of **[Jesus]**' Cross.
And you who were once estranged and hostile in mind, doing evil deeds,
[Jesus] has now reconciled in His fleshly body through death,
So as to present you holy and blameless and irreproachable
Before **Him**. Col. 1:13-22

[Jesus] is the reflection of God's Glory
And the exact imprint of God's very being
And **[Jesus]** sustains all things by His Powerful Word. Heb. 1:3

Therefore God also highly exalted **Jesus**
And gave **Jesus** the Name that is above every name
So that at the Name of **JESUS**
Every knee [shall] bow
In heaven and on earth and under the earth,
And every tongue [shall] confess
That JESUS CHRIST is LORD,
To the Glory of GOD the Father. Phil. 2:9-11 (The Greek word translated "should" here also means "shall" so that's what I wrote. The following verses actually use "shall.")

"...Every knee shall bow...and every tongue shall give praise to God." Rom. 14:11
"To Me every knee shall bow, every tongue shall swear." Is. 45:23

God's Glory shall fill the whole earth. Let's fill our heart with this Glorious truth until we are bursting with longing for that day.
As I live...all the earth shall be filled with the Glory of the Lord.... Nu. 14:21
The earth will be filled with the knowledge of the Glory of the Lord as the waters cover the sea. Hab 2:14
They shall not hurt or destroy on all My holy mountain; for the earth will be full of the knowledge of the Lord as the waters cover the sea. Is. 11:9
For it is God who commanded LIGHT to shine out of darkness...to give the LIGHT of the knowledge of the GLORY of GOD in the Face of JESUS CHRIST. II Cor. 4:6

Prayer of Worship

Nov. 14, 01

Jesus, I am in awe that You who "rides on the clouds," and on the "wind as wings," who "wraps Yourself with Light as a garment," whose presence causes earthquakes and lightning and "oaks to whirl," would call me to be near You, to sit at Your feet and listen to You, to soak in every Word You speak to me, and to minister to You with my ointment. I pray I will be filled with overwhelming adoration for YOU—with undying, unquenchable, eternal adoration—for You my Redeemer, Savior, Bridegroom, Friend, Master, Lord—my JESUS.

Devote yourselves to prayer, keeping alert in it with thanksgiving.
                                                            Colossians 4:2

God's
Plan and Purpose
Shall Stand

Let's strengthen our faith still more by meditating upon God's unshakeable plan. Read this section out loud. Then meditate on it.

I am God, and there is no one like Me, declaring the end from the beginning and from ancient times things not yet done, saying, "My purpose shall stand, and I will fulfill My intention," ...I have spoken, and I will bring it to pass; I have planned, and I will do it. Is. 46:9-11

I the Lord will speak the Word that I speak; and it will be fulfilled. It will no longer be delayed…. None of My Words will be delayed any longer, but the Word that I speak will be fulfilled, says the Lord God. Ezek. 12:25,28

The former things I declared long ago, they went out from My mouth and I made them known; then suddenly I did them and they came to pass. Is. 48:3

As I have designed so shall it be, and as I have planned so shall it come to pass. Is. 14:24

For I have spoken, I have purposed; I have not relented nor will I turn back. Jer. 4:28

This is the plan that is planned concerning the whole earth and this is the hand that is stretched out over all the nations. For the Lord of hosts has planned and who will annul it? His hand is stretched out and who will turn it back? Is. 24:26-27

Consider the work of God; who can make straight what He has made crooked? Ecc. 7:13

The human mind may devise many plans, but it is the purpose of the Lord that will be established. Prov. 19:21

The days are near when every vision will be fulfilled. Ezek. 12:23 NIV

The Lord will not turn back until He has executed and accomplished the intents of His mind. Jer. 32:20

None of His Words fall to the ground. I Sam. 3:19

Have you not heard that I determined it from long ago? I planned from days of old what now I bring to pass…. Is. 37:26

I the Lord have spoken, and I will surely do these things. Nu. 14:35 NIV

I the Lord have spoken. I will accomplish it. Ezek. 17:24

I the Lord have spoken; the time is coming, I will act. I will not refrain. Ezek. 24:14

I am the Lord, in its time I will accomplish it quickly. Is. 60:22

Who can command and have it done, if the Lord has not ordained it? Lam. 3:37

I, the Lord, have spoken, and I will do it. Ezek. 36:36

It has come! It has happened, says the Lord God. This is the day of which I have spoken. Ezek. 39:8

Everyone…will fear because of the plan that the Lord of hosts is planning. Is. 19:17

The Lord of hosts has planned it. Is. 23:9

He has made known…His…plan for the fullness of time…who accomplishes all things according to His counsel and will…for the praise of His Glory. Eph. 1:9-11,14

The plans of the Lord stand firm forever; the purposes of His heart through all generations. Ps. 33:11

Record verses you find on this subject in this space.

Prayer About God's Plan

Father, Your purpose shall stand. You have spoken and You will do it. O Adonai, we agree with You in prayer. Let Your plan come to pass. We want only Your Will to be done. O Father, execute Your intent. Let no other plan prosper.

Bring Your suddenly. Act upon Your Words. Let none of them fall to the ground. Fulfill all that You have spoken. Accomplish it. Make Your Word and Your Will reign supreme here on earth and let Your Glory shine forth.

Sept. 22, '05

And God who searches the heart, knows what is the mind of the Spirit, because the Spirit intercedes...according to the will of God. Romans 8:27

The Elim Bible Institute professor, Sister Sylvia Evans, said, "The Holy Spirit knows His own mind and intention and purpose. He knows where He is taking us; what He is going to birth out of all this. He is the Eternal Spirit. He is in the now of all the past and all the future. He knows the end from the beginning. From the beginning He knows the end. The "end" is the purpose—the ultimate purpose. He makes intercession according to the Will of God. His alignment is always with the Will of God. He is always going to pray God into the situation."

So, please pray through us, Holy Spirit!!!!

(Write another prayer here, if you'd like.)

I am watching over My Word to perform it. Jeremiah 1:12

The appointed time has come. Psalms 102:13

Know the History:

End Time Prophesies
That Have Been Fulfilled

I include this section to show us that Biblical prophecies do come to pass; that the prophecies listed in this book *will also* come to pass.

The Bubonic Plague/Black Death in the Middle Ages

The earth lies polluted under its inhabitants; for they have transgressed laws, violated the statutes, broken the everlasting covenant. Therefore a curse devours the earth, and its inhabitants suffer their guilt; therefore the inhabitants of the earth dwindled, and few people are left. Is. 24:6 {Some towns were completely wiped out during that time.}

It's rider's name was death, and Hades with him; they were given authority over one-fourth of the earth, to kill with...pestilence, and by the wild animals.... Rev. 6:8 {About one-fourth of the world's population died from the plague that was spread by rats.}

Israel's Disbursement

If you do not diligently observe all the Words...in this Book, ...then...the Lord will scatter you among all peoples, from one end of the earth to the other; .... Among these nations you shall find no ease, no resting place.... Deut. 28:58,64-65

I the Lord have spoken, and I will do it. I will scatter you among the nations and disperse you through the countries, and I will purge your filthiness out of you. And I shall be profaned through you in the sight of the nations; and you shall know that I am the Lord.
Ezek. 22:14-16

When you have had children and children's children and become complacent in the land, if you act corruptly...doing evil in the sight of the Lord your God and provoking Him to anger. I will call heaven and earth to witness against you today that you will soon utterly perish from the land.... The Lord will scatter you among the peoples, only a few of you will be left among the nations where the Lord will lead you. From there you will seek the Lord your God, and you will find Him if you search after Him with all your heart and soul.... In your distress, when all these things have happened to you in time to come, you will return to the Lord your God and heed Him. Deut. 4:25-27, 29-30

I scattered them among the nations, yet in far countries they shall remember Me.
Zech.10:9

The Great Depression

A quart of wheat for a day's pay, and three quarts of barley for a day's pay. Rev.6:6 {This happened in America during the Depression. People had to grow their own food because they couldn't afford to buy it. In China before Communism they were carrying their paper money around in wheelbarrows just to buy eggs and bread.}

The Holocaust

"Woe to those who are pregnant and to those who are nursing infants in those days! Pray that your flight may not be in winter or on a Sabbath. For at that time there will be great suffering, such as has not been from the beginning of the world until now, no, and never will be. And if those days had not been cut short, no one would be saved; but for the sake of the elect those days will be cut short." Matt. 24:20-22 {This has to be for the Holocaust, because the Holocaust was the worst suffering for the Jews ever in history. It was terrible when Rome crushed Jerusalem in 70AD, but the Holocaust was worse. Maybe it is a two-fold prophecy—for both.}

He [God] has confirmed His Words, which He spoke against us and against our rulers, by bringing upon us a calamity so great that what has been done against Jerusalem has never before been done under the whole heaven.... The Lord kept watch over this calamity until He brought it upon us. Dan. 9:12

"The end has come upon my people Israel; I will never again pass them by. The songs of the temple shall become wailings in that day," says the Lord God; "the dead bodies shall be many, cast out in every place. Be silent!" Amos 8:2-3 (Exactly what happened!)

I will turn your feasts into mourning, and all your songs into lamentation; I will bring sackcloth on all loins, and baldness on every head; I will make it like the mourning for an only son, and the end of it like a bitter day. Amos 8:10

O My poor people put on sackcloth, and roll in ashes; make mourning as for an only child, most bitter lamentation: for suddenly the destroyer will come upon us. Jer. 6:26

And Isaiah cries out concerning Israel, "Though the number of the Children of Israel were like the sand of the sea, only a remnant of them will be saved; for the Lord will execute His sentence on the earth quickly and decisively." As Isaiah predicted, "if the Lord of hosts had not left survivors to us, we would have fared like Sodom and been made like Gomorrah."
Rom. 9:27-29

They shall be like...smoke from a window. Hos. 13:3

For though Your people Israel were like the sands of the sea, only a remnant of them will return. Destruction is decreed, overflowing with righteousness. Is. 10:22

Although once you were as numerous as the stars in heaven, you shall be left few in number, because you did not obey the Lord your God. Deut. 28:62

They shall pass through the sea of distress. Zech. 10:11

In the morning you shall say, "If only it were evening!" and at the evening you shall say, "If only it were morning!" — because of the dread that your heart shall feel and the sights that your eyes shall see. Deut. 28:67

See, a day is coming for the Lord, when the plunder taken from you will be divided in your midst. For I will gather all the nations against Jerusalem to battle, and the city shall be taken and the houses looted and the women raped; half the city shall go into exile, but the rest of the people shall not be cut off. Zech. 14:1-2 {This is just what happened in the Holocaust. Their houses were looted, women raped, and no nation came to help. All were against them. Even America turned their escaping ships away! God help us!}

In the whole land, declares the Lord, two-thirds will be struck down and perish; yet one-third will be left in it. This third I will bring into the fire; I will refine them like silver and test them like gold. Zech. 13:7-9 NIV

In Mount Zion and in Jerusalem there shall be those who escape, as the Lord has said, and among the survivors shall be those whom the Lord calls. Joel 2:23

Israel's Wars: Independence, 1948; Six Day, 1967; Yom Kippur, 1972

The day is surely coming, says the Lord, when I will restore the fortunes of My people, Israel and Judah, says the Lord, and I will bring them back to the Land that I gave to their ancestors and they shall take possession of it. Jer. 30:3

Before she was in labor she gave birth; before her pain came upon her she delivered a son. Who has heard of such a thing: Who has seen such things: Shall a land be born in one day? Shall a nation be delivered in one moment? Yet as soon as Zion was in labor she delivered her children. Is. 66:8

And the land of Judah will become a terror to the Egyptians. Is. 19:17 (Egypt was shaken up when they lost the 1948 war with Israel.)

Then the Lord will go forth and fight against those nations as when He fights on a day of battle. Zech. 14:3

The US and the UN trying to get peace for Israel

They have treated the wound of my people carelessly, saying, "Peace, peace," when there is no peace. Jer. 6:14

They have divided My land. Joel 3:2

We look for peace, but find no good, ...the whole land quakes. They come and devour...the city and those who live in it. See I am letting snakes loose among you, adders that cannot be charmed, and they shall bite you, says the Lord. Jer. 8:15 (Terrorists!)

The World Believing in Evolution

First of all you must understand this, that in the last days scoffers will come, scoffing and indulging in their own lusts and saying, "Where is the promise of His coming? For ever since our ancestors died, all things continue as they were from the beginning of creation!" **They deliberately ignore this fact**, that by the Word of God heavens existed long ago and an earth was formed out of water. I Pet. 2:3-6

The Sixties in America, and Since
Famine of the Word of God:

The time is surely coming, says the Lord God, when I will send a famine on the land; not a famine of bread, or a thirst for water, but of hearing the Words of the Lord. They shall wander from sea to sea, and from north to east; they shall run to and fro, seeking the Word of the Lord, but they shall not find it. In that day the beautiful young women and the young men shall faint for thirst. Amos 8:11-13

The Word of the Lord is to them an object of scorn Jer. 6:10

{Doesn't this sound exactly like the Sixties? Young people went from "North" America to India in the "east" to seek answers from gurus. They wandered "to and fro," from "sea to sea" and they did not find it, instead they began to scorn the Bible and they established the New Age religion. This happened during my childhood and it makes me cry just to think about it.}

See, the Name of the Lord comes from far away, burning with His anger...to place on the jaws of the peoples a bridle that leads them astray. Is. 30:28

Thus says the Lord concerning the prophets who lead My people astray.... Therefore it shall be night to you, without vision and darkness to you, without revelation. The sun shall go down upon the prophets, and the day shall be black over them; the seers shall be disgraced; ...they shall all cover their lips, for there is no answer from God. Micah 3:5-8

{It was in the sixties that, the American society began to look down on and mock preachers and Bible Believers.]

Ah, you who are heroes in drinking wine and valiant at mixing drink. Is. 5:22

Ah, you...who linger in the evening to be inflamed by wine [and drugs], whose feasts consist of lyre and harp, tambourine and flute and wine, but who do not regard the deeds of the Lord, or see the work of His hands! Therefore My people...are dying of hunger, and their multitude is parched with thirst. Is. 5:11-13 {Our young people are dying of hunger for the Bread of Life, and of thirst for the Living Water. (See Amos 8 above.)}

Rebellion and immorality:

The youth will be insolent to the elder, and the base to the honorable. Is. 3:5

Father and mother are treated with contempt. Ezek. 22:7

Oh, rebellious children, says the Lord, who carry out a plan, but not Mine; who make an alliance, but against My will, adding sin to sin. Is. 30:1

You have despised the rod, and all discipline. Ezek. 21:10

God is pronouncing all the following things as punishing judgments over people:

My people—children are their oppressors, and women rule over them. {The feminist movement!} O My people, your leaders mislead you, and confuse the course of your paths. Is. 3:12 {The feminists lies *have* misled and confused this nation!}

And I will make boys their princes, and babes shall rule over them. Is. 3:4 {I first noticed this when Clinton was our young president and was behaving like a wild youth. It was a poignant verse to me.}

Ah, you who call evil good and good evil, who put darkness for light and light for darkness...! Is. 5:20 {I was shocked when I first came across this verse because it was when Michael Jackson had just released his song, "Bad, Bad, Bad," and teenagers were starting to use the word "bad" to mean "good." Today this verse really does apply to our society! May God rescue us})

I will not punish your daughters when they ...commit adultery; for the men themselves go aside with whores. Hos. 4:14

Father and son go in to the same girl, so that My Holy Name is profaned. Amos 2:7 (On the TV show, *ER*, in 1995, or so, this was portrayed and treated as laughable.)

Their glory is in their shame. Phil. 3:19

You have despised My Holy things, and profaned My Sabbaths. Ezek. 22:8

They have no distinction between the Holy and the common. Ezek. 22:26

The best of them is like a brier, the most upright of them is like a thorn. Mic. 7:4

A fool will no longer be called noble, nor a villain said to be honorable. Is. 32:5 {So before this a fool *was* called noble. Is that not true in America now? Aren't most of our celebrities and political leaders actually fools?}

About the Liberals and Most of Societies Leaders Today:

Ah, you who are wise in your own eyes, and shrewd in your own sight! Is. 5:21

They have rejected the...Lord, and...have been led astray by...lies. Amos 2:4

Those who led this people led them astray, and those who were led by them were left in confusion. Is. 9:16

Their speech and their deeds are against the Lord, defying His glorious presence.
Is. 3:8

They have rejected the instruction of the Lord of hosts, and have despised the Word of the Holy One. Is. 5:24

The Word of the Lord is to them an object of scorn; they take no pleasure in it. Jer. 6:10

Then [they] shall say, "Hush! We must not mention the Name of the Lord. Amos 6:10 {No mention of God is allowed in many places in America today!}

The powerful dictate what they desire; thus they pervert justice. Mic. 7:3

"Give heed to the sound of the trumpet!" But they said, "We will not give heed." Jer. 6:17 {They are refusing to believe in or heed the trumpet of the rapture!}

Other things that have come to pass in America:

The Lord our God has...given us **poisoned water to drink**, because we have sinned against the Lord. Jer. 8.14:

Therefore thus says the Lord of hosts concerning the prophets: "I am going to make them eat wormwood, and give them **poisoned water to drink**; for...ungodliness has spread throughout the land." Jer. 23.15 {The first time I noticed these verses (in 1995 or so) there were news stories in America about bad-water like the two young sisters who got terribly sick from a drinking fountain at a county fair. I was shocked to see that it could be God's judgment on our nation! Soon people started carrying bottled water with them everywhere. Today water bottles are considered completely normal. We view our tap water as poisoned. Is God's Word coming to pass or what?}

From the least to the greatest of them, everyone is greedy. Jer. 6:13

Ah, you who join house to house, who add field to field, until there is room for no one but you, and you are left to live alone in the midst of the land! ...Therefore the anger of the Lord was kindled against His people, and He stretched out His hand against them. Is. 5:8,25

Do not learn the way of the nations, or be dismayed at the signs of the heavens; for the nations are dismayed at them. Jer. 10:2 (Acid rain! Ozone layer! Global warming! Global ice age predicted in the 1970's!)

What the wicked dread will come upon them. Prov. 10:24

Alas for those...who trust in chariots because they are many and in horsemen because they are very strong, but do not look to the Holy one...or consult the Lord! Is. 31:1

This is the nation that did not obey the voice of the Lord their God, and did not accept discipline; **truth has perished**.... The Lord has rejected and forsaken the generation that provoked His wrath. Jer. 7:28,29 {The Truth is perishing in this country!}

Because they have not given heed to My Words; and as for My teaching, they have rejected it.... Therefore thus says the Lord: See, I am laying before this people stumbling blocks against which they shall stumble; parents and children together, {Harry Potter!} neighbor and friend shall perish. Jer. 6:19,21 {The neighbors and friends perish because we, in our straying from God, have not brought them to the Lord.}

They have rejected the Word of the Lord...therefore I will give their wives to others. Jer.8:9 {Our divorce rate!}

They acted shamefully...yet they were not at all ashamed, they did not know how to blush. Therefore they shall fall at the time when I punish them...says the Lord. Jer. 8:12 {This has been true in America since the sixties. We don't know how to blush. In fact, we are often proud of what should make us feel ashamed. Many of us have been falling already for many reasons: cancer, AIDS, disaster etc. Let's pray that the next phrase in the verse doesn't also happen to us: *They shall be overthrown.*}

Why has this people turned away in perpetual backsliding? ...I have given heed and listened, but they do not speak honestly; no one repents...saying, "What have I done!" All of them turn to their own course. Jer. 8:5 {There has not been an attitude of repentance in America for a long, long time.}

When I wanted to gather them, says the Lord, there are (sic.) no grapes on the vine, nor figs on the fig tree; even the leaves are withered and what I gave them has passed away from them. Jer. 8:13 {The Lord gave America so much: religious freedom, solid teaching in the Truth of the Bible, a moral, Christian culture, peace, wealth and power. But slowly now these things are all eroding away.}

Can't Buy or Sell

And it was allowed to give breath to the image of the beast so that the image of the beast could even speak and cause those who would not worship the image of the beast to be killed. Also it causes all, both small and great, both rich and poor, both free and slave, to be marked on the right hand or the forehead, so that no one can buy or sell who does not have the mark, that is, the name of the beast. Rev. 13:15-17

Most people believe this is still to be fulfilled in the future. I am not a Bible scholar, but I believe it has already come to pass in many places in the earth.

The "beast" can be interpreted as a kingdom. Daniel was told, "*The fourth **beast** is a fourth kingdom that will appear on the earth.*" Dan. 7:23 niv

In the communist USSR "kingdom," people could not buy or sell if they did not agree with the communist philosophy, and they were killed if they chose to worship God instead of Communism. The same was true with Naziism in Germany in the 1940's; and with Catholicism in Europe in the Middle Ages.

It is still happening today in countries like Laos, North Korea, Iran, and even in communist China. A young Christian couple is in prison in China today (March 2006) who wanted to print and sell Christian literature, namely, *Experiencing God* by Henry Blackaby. (See *Voice of the Martyrs*, Feb. 06.) In many Muslim communities those known to be Christians cannot buy or sell, and both converts and missionaries are being martyred. Do we want to tell all these people who have suffered, and are suffering, that this prophesy hasn't come to pass yet just because it hasn't touched us?

You might say this couldn't be the fulfillment of this prophecy because no one has been required to have a name or number written on their hand or forehead. Well, that part of the prophecy may not need to be taken literally. In the very next verse, in Rev. 14:1 it says, "*And there was the Lamb...and with Him were one hundred forty-four thousand who had His Name and His Father's Name **written on their foreheads***." The Christians had Jesus' Name and God's Name *written* on their foreheads. If we are going to take the writing of the beast's name literally, then we should take this verse literally, and we should all get to work tattooing our foreheads.

So, perhaps this prophecy has already come to pass on a certain level. There are other prophecies that have been fulfilled more than once, for example, Daniel's about the desecration of the temple, and the ones about Israel returning to her land. But remember, I am not a prophecy expert. I'm just giving you something to ponder.

They hunt each other with nets.... Put no trust in a friend, have no confidence in a loved one; guard the doors of your mouth from her who lies in your embrace. Mic. 7:2,5 This Scripture has also come true in the countries I mentioned above. I saw it in China in 1980. People did not even trust their closest friends.

And they overcame him [the enemy] by the Blood...and by the Word.

Revelation 12:11

Let the weakling say, "I am a warrior." Joel 3:10

RECEIVE YOUR ARTILLERY:

Prayer Warfare
Scriptures

Here are some Scriptures that explain what spiritual warfare is. Let's read them aloud to make our faith divinely powerful, and to inspire us for battle. (Remember the word "enemy" *does not mean* "people," but the "devil and all his demons." Even if a verse says "people" or "nations" think "the enemy.")

Who is doing the fighting:

The Son of God was revealed for this purpose, to destroy the works of the devil (NRSV). The reason the Son came was to destroy the devil's work (NIV). I Jn. 3:8

Rally to us wherever you hear the sound of the trumpet. Our God will fight for us. Neh. 4:20

It is the Lord God who fights for you as He promised. One of you puts to flight a thousand. Josh. 23:10 and Lev. 26:8

Wait for the Lord; be strong and let your heart take courage; wait for the Lord! Ps. 27:14

O God, Your chariots are tens of thousands and thousands of thousands! Ps. 68:17

The mountain was full of horses and chariots of fire all around. II Kings 6:17

Do not fear or be dismayed at this great multitude; for the battle is not yours but God's. II Chron. 20:15

Do not be afraid. Stand firm and see the deliverance that the Lord will accomplish for you today. Ex. 14:13

Do not fear them, for it is the Lord your God who fights for you. Deut. 3:22

Do not lose heart or be afraid or panic or be in dread for it is the Lord your God who goes before you to fight for you against your enemies, to give you victory. Deut. 20:3-4

(Sometimes the Lord wants us to fight with Him.)

Do not be afraid of them. Remember the Lord, who is great and awesome, and fight. Neh. 4:14

(Other times all He wants from us is to watch in reverential awe as He accomplishes His purpose.)

The Lord will fight for you and you have only to keep still. Ex. 14:14

If My people would but listen to Me…and would follow My ways how quickly would I subdue their enemies and turn My hand against their foes! Those who hate the Lord would cringe before Him, and their punishment would last forever. Ps. 81:13-15 NIV

Then you shall call, and the Lord will answer; you shall cry and the Lord will say, "Here I am." Is. 58:9 NKJV

Your [God's] hand will find out all Your enemies; Your right hand will find out those who hate You. You will make all the enemies like a fiery furnace when You appear. The Lord will swallow them up in His wrath, and fire will consume them. You will destroy their offspring from the earth…from among humankind. If they plan evil against You, if they devise mischief, they will not succeed. For You will put them to flight…with Your bows. Be exalted, O Lord, in Your strength. We will sing and praise Your power. Ps. 21:8-12

[Speaking to the enemy] Band together…and be dismayed. Take counsel together, but it shall be brought to naught; speak a word, but it will not stand, for God is with us. Is. 8:9,10

Be wise in what is good and guileless in what is evil. The God of peace will shortly crush satan under your feet. Rom. 16:19-20

The position of authority from which we are fighting:

And [God] seated Him [Jesus] at His right hand in the heavenly places **far** above **all** rule and authority and power and dominion and above every name that is named... and has put all things under His feet and has made Him the head over all things. Eph. 1:20-22

He has made us alive together with Christ...and raised us with Him and seated us with Him in the heavenly places in Christ Jesus. Eph. 2:6

[Jesus] said to them, "I watched satan fall from heaven like a flash of lightning. See, I have given you authority...over **all** the power of the enemy." Lk. 10:18-19

With the eyes of your heart enlightened,... **know**...what is the immeasurable greatness of His power for us who believe. Eph. 1:18,19

For the One who is in you is greater than the one who is in the world. I Jn. 4:4

Now my head is lifted up above my enemies all around me. Ps. 27:6

Who we are fighting:

For our struggle is not against flesh and blood, but against the rulers, against the authorities, against the [NRSV: cosmic] powers in this dark world, and against spiritual forces of evil in the heavenly realm [NRSV: places]. Eph. 6:12 NIV

The whole world is under the power of the evil one. I Jn. 5:19

The god of this world has blinded the minds of the unbelievers to keep them from seeing the Light of the Glory of Christ. II Cor. 4:3-4

...in which you once lived, following the course of this world, following the ruler of the power of the air, the spirit that is now at work among those who are disobedient. Eph. 2:2

Some will abandon the faith and follow deceiving spirits and things taught by demons. I Tim. 4:13

Our Weapons:

They have conquered him [the enemy] by the Blood of the Lamb and by the **Word**.... Rev. 12:11

Is not My **Word** like fire, says the Lord, and like a hammer that breaks a rock in pieces? Jer. 23:29

Jesus said, "My kingdom is not of this world." Jn. 18:36 NIV

For the weapons we fight with [NKJV: of our warfare] are not the weapons of the world. On the contrary, they have **Divine Power** to demolish strongholds. II Cor. 10:4

Therefore take up the whole armor of God, so that you may be able to withstand on that evil day. Eph. 6:13

Take...the **sword of the Spirit**, which is the **Word of God**. Pray in the Spirit at all times. Eph. 6:17-18

Let the high praises of God be in their throats and two-edged **swords** [God's Word] in their hands, to execute vengeance on the nations and punishment on the peoples, to bind their kings with fetters and their nobles with chains of iron. Ps. 149:6-8

"...**Say** to this mountain [the enemy], 'Be removed....'" Matt. 21:21 NKJV

"...**Say** to this mulberry tree [the enemy], 'Be uprooted....'" Lk. 17:6 NIV

From His mouth comes a sharp **sword** with which to strike down the nations. Rev. 19:15

And the rest were killed by the **sword** of the Rider on the horse, the **sword** that came from His mouth. Rev. 19:21

Our Weapons (cont.):

You are My war club, My weapon of battle: with you I smash nations; with you I destroy kingdoms. Jer. 51:20-21

[Jesus said,] "I came to bring fire to the earth and how I wish it were already kindled." Lk. 12:49

Statements of Faith:

For whatever is born of God overcomes the world. And this is the victory that overcomes the world, even our faith. Who is it that conquers the world but the one who believes that Jesus is the Son of God. I Jn. 5:4-5

My eyes have seen the downfall of my enemies. My ears have heard the doom of my evil assailants. Ps. 92:10-11

I will look in triumph on my enemy. Ps. 118:7

Though an army encamp against me to devour my flesh, my heart shall not fear; though war rise up against me, yet I will be confident. My adversaries and foes shall stumble and fall. Ps. 27:3,2

God gives us training and help:

Blessed be the Lord, my Rock, who trains my hand for war, and my fingers for battle. Ps. 144:1

The weapons of our warfare are not...human, but they have **Divine Power**. II Cor. 10:4

It is You who light my lamp; the Lord, my God, lights up my darkness. By You I can crush a troop, and by my God I can leap over a wall.... He trains my hands for war, so that my arms can bend a bow of bronze. You have given me the shield of Your salvation, and Your right hand has supported me. Ps. 18:28-29,34-35

Let us stand up together. Who are my adversaries? Let them confront me. It is the Lord who helps me. Is. 49:8

The Lord is my Rock, my Fortress, and my Deliverer, ...my Rock, in whom I take refuge, ...my Shield, ...my Stronghold. Ps. 18:1-3

The Lord is the Stronghold of my life; of whom shall I be afraid? Ps. 27:1

He gives power to the faint and strengthens the powerless. Is. 40:29

Do not fear for I am with you, do not be afraid for I am your God; I will strengthen you, I will help you, I will uphold you with my victorious right hand. Yes, all who are incensed against you shall be ashamed and disgraced; those who strive against you...shall perish.... Those who war against you shall be as nothing at all. Is. 41:10-12

Do not fear, you worm..., you insect...! I will help you, says the Lord; your Redeemer is the Holy One of Israel. Now, I will make of you a threshing sledge, sharp, new, and having teeth; you shall thresh the mountains and crush them, and you shall make the hills like chaff. You shall winnow them and the wind shall carry them away, and the tempest shall scatter them. Then you shall rejoice in the Lord; in the Holy One of Israel you shall glory.... So all may see and know, all may consider and understand, that the hand of the Lord has done this. Is. 41:14-16, 20

I will go before you and level the mountains, I will break in pieces the doors of bronze and cut through the bars of iron. Is. 45:2

The Spirit helps us in our weakness...to pray...with sighs too deep for words. Rom. 8:26

We do not know how to pray as we ought, but that very Spirit intercedes...according to the will of God. Rom. 8:26,27

It is Christ Jesus, who died, yes, who was raised, who is at the right hand of God, who indeed intercedes for us. Rom. 8:34

God's Strategy:

Surely the Lord...does nothing without revealing His secret to His servants, the prophets. Amos 3:7

The Lord has spoken, who can but prophesy? Amos 3:8

Proclaim to the strongholds.... An adversary shall surround the land, and strip you of your defense; and your strongholds shall be plundered. Amos 3:9,11

Foreigners [the enemies] lost heart, and came trembling out of their strongholds. Ps. 18:45

I will send a fire...and it will devour the strongholds. Amos 1:4

For the weapons of our warfare are not carnal but **mighty in God** for pulling down strongholds, casting down arguments and every high thing that exalts itself against the knowledge of God. II Cor. 10:4-5 NKJV

They have divine power to demolish strongholds. We demolish arguments and every pretension that sets itself up against the knowledge of God, and we take captive every thought to make it obedient to Christ. II Cor. 10:4-5

I appoint you over nations and kingdoms to uproot and tear down, to destroy and overthrow [The Hebrew also means: demolish], to build and to plant. Jer. 1:10 NIV

Promises:

Wait for the Lord and keep His way and He will exalt you to inherit the land; and you will look on the destruction of the wicked. Ps. 37:34

Your enemies will cower before you and you will trample down their high places. Deut. 33:29

All the hosts of heaven shall rot away, and the skies shall roll up like a scroll. {This is the second heaven where the demons are.} All their hosts shall wither like a leaf withering on a vine or fruit withering on a fig tree. Is. 34:4 (Jesus withered a fig tree and told us we can do the same and more! See Matt. 21:18-22)

And you shall tread down the wicked, for they will be ashes under the soles of your feet, on the day when I act, says the Lord of hosts. Mal. 4:3

Prayers from Scripture:

You, Lord, You rescue us (NIV) from those too strong for us.... You have seen, O Lord, do not be silent! ...Vindicate us in Your righteousness (NIV).... Do not let them rejoice.... Do not let them say to themselves, "Aha, we have our heart's desire." Do not let them say, "We have swallowed you up." Ps. 35:10,22,24-25 NRSV

Contend, O Lord, with those who contend with me. Fight against those who fight against me.... Let them be turned back and confounded who devise evil.... Let them be like chaff before the wind, with the angel of the Lord driving them on. Let their way be dark and slippery, with the angel of the Lord pursuing them. Ps. 35:1-6

In Your steadfast love, cut off [NIV: silence] my enemies and destroy my adversaries for I am Your servant. Ps. 143:12

Victory:

I will sing to the Lord for He has triumphed gloriously...the Lord is a warrior; the Lord is His name.... Your right hand, O Lord, glorious in power—Your right hand, O Lord, shattered the enemy. In the greatness of Your Majesty You overthrew Your adversaries; You sent out Your fury, it consumed them like stubble.... They trembled; pangs seized [them]. Terror and dread fell upon them; by the might of Your arm, they became still as stone.... The Lord will reign forever and ever. Ex. 15:15-18

Your help has made me great. You gave me a wide place for my steps under me, and my feet did not slip. I pursued my enemies and overtook them; and did not turn back until they were consumed. I struck them down, so that they were not able to rise; they fell under my feet. For You girded me with strength for the battle; You made my assailants sink under me. You made my enemies turn their backs to me, and those...I destroyed.... I beat them fine, like dust before the wind; I cast them out like the mire of the streets.... [They] came cringing to me...[they] lost heart, and came trembling out of their strongholds.... Blessed be my Rock, and exalted be the God of my salvation, the God who gave me vengeance and subdued [them] under me; who delivered me from my enemies; indeed, You exalted me above my adversaries.

Ps. 18:35-48

(Write more verses on this subject here.)

Lou Engle's thoughts on spiritual warfare:

God is not randomly or haphazardly crashing into human history. He has initiated rules of engagement for His break-ins and breakthroughs. He does nothing until He can find a partner on earth with whom He can share His secrets and His intercessions. His servants, the prophets, receive His message and through proclamation, fasting, and prayer, bring to earth what God is doing in Heaven. "Thy Kingdom come, Thy will be done on earth as it is in heaven." Earthlings must pray God's will into the earth.

Without these highly esteemed "earth beings" (remember Daniel), God will not intervene into the injustice and suffering of mankind. Therefore, God looks for a man or woman, a human being with feet planted firmly on the earth, ...who demands in prayer on earth what God demands in heaven. This is God's breathtaking view of man and history. We are called to shape history through prayer and fasting, and millions of these earth beings are stepping into their heavenly calling. It is all headed to the mountain of the Lord, Mt. Zion, where Christ Himself will take up His throne and rule through His King priest ministry.

From www.facedown40.com/journal: Sunday, 19 March 2006. (Used by permission.)

Prayer about Spiritual Warfare

Nov. 30, '05

[Prayer from Ps. 18 (p. 48 and 50)]

Yes, Jesus, teach me to do spiritual warfare against the kingdom of darkness. Gird me with strength for the battles. Train me to bend Your awesomely beautiful bow of bronze. Help me to leap over the enemy's wall. Give me a wide place for my steps so my feet don't slip. Make the enemies of Your Gospel obey the voice of Your Words. Make them lose heart and come cringing and trembling out of their strongholds at the mention of Your Name. Help me to pursue them and overtake them. Help me not to turn back or quit until they are consumed. Help me to strike all Your enemies down so they cannot rise. Make my assailants sink under me. Make them turn their backs so I can destroy them. Help me to crush the devil's troops who are trying to trample Your Kingdom. Help me to beat them fine like dust before the wind. Help me to cast them out like the mire of the streets to be swept away into the fiery furnace.

I came to bring fire to the earth and how I wish it were already kindled. Lk. 12:49

O Jesus, You came to kindle a fire and You want it to burn and burn and grow into a raging fire that takes over the earth. O let it burn, Jesus. Let it burn!!! Pentecost was only the kindling of that fire!! O let Your fire burn bright, Jesus—brighter and brighter and brighter. Let Your fire take over the earth. Let Your fire take over religious spirits and pride and arrogance. Let it take over all churches—Your True fire, Jesus!! Let it take over Hollywood and TV and all movies and bookstores. Let it take over the Muslim world until they are all on fire for You!

In *The Three Battlegrounds* on page 45, Francis Frangipane (Arrow Publications, Cedar Rapids, IA, 1989) says, "Most Christians only engage in spiritual warfare with the hope of either relieving present distresses or attaining a 'normal existence' but it is to make us Christ-like."

Yes, that was me, Jesus. That was all I wanted it for, too. And I desperately needed it! But now I believe spiritual warfare is also for a much higher purpose. Yes, it is to bring us fully into You, Jesus—fully surrendered to You. We all need it for that. But it is for even more! It is to rise higher and higher in Your kingdom until we join You in doing Spiritual warfare in the world to set people free, to set the world free from the strongholds and powers of all the enemies of the Kingdom of Heaven.

Jesus, I want to go higher and higher in this. I want to go as high as You ever want to take anyone. As high as You want to take *me*. Holy Spirit, take me higher and higher until I reach the "height and depth and width and breadth" of Spirituality and of Spiritual warfare. Set me on FIRE for You, Jesus. Help me spread Your FIRE!!

Wait for the Lord! (Ps. 27:14). Yes, Jesus, I wait for You. I do not want to fight without You. I will only fight when You are fighting. The battle is Yours. Help me to wait for You, Jesus. If I wait I will never be fighting alone. I will be joining You and Your heavenly hosts!

If my people would but listen to Me... (Ps. 81:13). O Jesus, help me—help us to listen to You and follow You so we do not hinder our own victory! Help the world to listen to You and follow You so You can quickly subdue all evil and banish it from this earth (even from churches).

Jan. 2, '06

Happy {Blessed, Shalomed!} *are the people...who walk, O Lord, in the LIGHT of Your countenance* {—Your presence—Your FACE!!!}; *they exult in Your Name **all day long** [!] and extol Your righteousness.... My hand shall always remain with him. My arm shall strengthen him. The enemy shall not outwit him. The wicked shall not humble him. I will crush his foes before him and strike down those who hate him.... He shall cry to Me, "You are my Father, my God and the Rock of my salvation."* Ps. 89:15,21-23,26

O Father, O Jesus, my Redeemer, my Rock of Salvation, please let this come to pass for me. Help me walk in Your LIGHT—the Light of Your FACE and Your PRESENCE—and exult and extol You all day long. Be my strength and my shield. Make me mighty in You, Jesus. Keep Your hand with me and strengthen me with Your arm. Don't let the enemy outwit me, Jesus, or humble me or weaken me or make me shrink back. Please crush the enemy and strike him down. Amen!

Dec. 7, '05

Those who became believers confessed and disclosed their practices. A number of those who practiced **magic** *collected their books and burned them publicly...50,000 silver coins* [worth] [!!]. *So the* **Word of the Lord grew mightily and prevailed** [!!]. Acts 19:18-20

A man name Demetrius, a silversmith...to the artisans...said, "Men, you know that we get our wealth from this business. You see and hear that not only in Ephesus but in almost the whole of Asia this Paul has persuaded and drawn away a considerable number of people.... There is danger not only that this trade of ours may come into disrepute but also that the great goddess Artemis will be scorned, ...she...that brought all Asia and the world to worship her. Acts 19:24-27

("All Asia and the world" meant big business and big $$$!)

O Heavenly Father, I pray that Your Truth will go forth until all the people of the whole world will confess and disclose their practices of magic and ungodliness and will burn all their books, DVD's, CD's, movies, etc. Praise You, Jesus. I pray it will come to pass **globally**, Jesus. May all Harry Potter things come into disrepute. May all New Age things, all demonic, and all evil practices become scorned until all the people making money from these things become worried like Demetrius did; until they become impoverished and must turn to You; until they must believe that You are the True, Living God; until they repent of using evil and deception to extort money from the masses and even from children!!!

Please, God, remove the cloud of deception from people—even church people!

Mar. 3, '05

Our small group leader said last night that Elisha's servant saw true reality!

"Do not be afraid, for there are more with us than there are with them." Then Elisha prayed: "O Lord, please open his eyes that he may see." So the Lord opened the eyes of the servant, and he saw; the mountain was full of horses and chariots of fire all around Elisha. II Kings 6:16-17

O Jesus, I want to see true reality. I want to see Your horses and chariots of FIRE!! Your reality is more real and true than what we see with our human eyes.

Mar. 22, '06

O Yeshua Adonai, send Your angels and Your hosts and Your chariots against the leaders of Islam and Jihad and terror. Find them, Yeshua. Route them out. May they cringe before You and come trembling out of their strongholds and may their doom last forever!!!

In Your Name, Yeshua, rescue the children from them, from the horrible, evil deception. Take away the pull that makes the young people strap themselves with bombs. Open their eyes to see the hideous lies and the fraud. Take away the attraction of it, Yeshua. Deliver them from their religion of anger and hatred and violence. May they all come to know the God who loves them and values their lives, who gave His Son's life to rescue them. Visit them in their dreams, Yeshua.

I pray, Yeshua, that the terrorists will no longer be able to find any more young people who will volunteer for the suicide bombings, or any more mothers who will give up their children for this. I demolish that huge, demonic stronghold in the Powerful Name of Yeshua Adonai!! May it come crashing down and fall into complete disrepute to all its masses of people. May all its power be annihilated in Yeshua's Holy Name! May it become ashes under our feet and be swept into the Lake of Fire by the Power of the Blood of Yeshua HaMashiach! Hallelujah! Amen!

(Write your own battling prayers here)
(And remember to use the verses in this section to write prayers for the other sections in this book.)

The mind of the righteous ponders. Proverbs 15:28

God's Ultimate Goal and Purpose

In final preparation we must make sure we align our hearts with God's. Even in His fierce judgments, God desires with all His heart that everyone on earth repent and turn to Him to experience His glorious, majestic, abiding presence. Let's meditate on these Scriptures that express God's heart until they are solidly planted in our being.

Have I any pleasure in the death of the wicked, says the Lord God, and not rather that they should turn from their ways and live? Ezek. 18:23

For I have no pleasure in the death of anyone, says the Lord God. Turn, then, and live. Ezek. 18:32

As I live, says the Lord God, I have no pleasure in the death of the wicked, but that the wicked turn from their ways and live, turn back, turn back from your evil ways; for why will you die? Ezek. 33:11

For the Lord does not reject forever. Although He causes grief, He will have compassion according to the abundance of His steadfast Love for He does not willingly afflict or grieve anyone. Lam. 3:31-33

The Lord is not slow...but is patient with you, **not wanting any to perish**, but **all** to come to repentance.... Regard the patience of our Lord as salvation. II Pet. 3:9,15

While God has overlooked the times of human ignorance, now He commands **all people everywhere** to **repent**, because He has fixed a day on which He will have the world judged in righteousness by [Jesus]. Acts 17:30-31

Turn to Me and be saved, all the ends of the earth! For I am God, and there is no other. Is. 45:22

Return to Me, says the Lord of hosts, and I will return to you. Zech. 1:3

In the latter days I will bring you against My land, **so that the nations may know Me**, when through you, O Gog, I display My Holiness before their eyes. Ezek. 38:16

So, I will display My greatness and My Holiness **and make Myself known** in the eyes of many nations. Then they shall know that I am the Lord. Ezek. 38:23

God our Savior...desires **everyone to be saved** and come to the knowledge of the Truth. I Tim. 2:4

Christ Jesus...gave Himself a ransom for **all**. I Tim. 2:6

It is all for God's sake and for His Glory. Let's continue our meditating.

Thus says the Lord God; It is **not for your sake**, O _____[*your name and your country's name*], that I am about to act, but **for the sake of My Holy Name,** which you have profaned among the nations to which you came. I will sanctify My great Name, ... and the **nations shall know** that I am the Lord, says the Lord God, when through you I display My holiness before their eyes...I will sprinkle clean water upon you, and you shall be clean.... A new heart I will give you, and a new spirit I will put within you.... Then you shall remember your evil ways, and your dealings that were not good; and you shall loathe yourselves for your iniquities and your abominable deeds. It is **not for your sake** that I will act, says the Lord God; let that be known to you. Be ashamed and dismayed for your ways, O_____. Ezek. 36:22-31

Now therefore, O our God, listen to the prayer of Your servant and to his supplication, and **for Your own sake**, Lord, let Your face shine upon [us].... We do not present our supplication before You on the ground of our righteousness, but on the ground of Your great mercies.... **For your own sake, O my God**, because Your city and Your people bear Your Name. Dan. 9:17,19

These next passages show the kind of repentance God desires. May the Lord receive what He desires from us and from all our cities and nations today.

Yet even now, says the Lord, return to Me with all your heart, with **fasting**, with **weeping**, and with **mourning**; rend your hearts.... Return to the Lord, your God, for He is gracious and merciful, slow to anger, and abounding in steadfast love, and relents from punishing. Who knows whether He will not turn and relent, and leave a blessing behind Him?
Joel 2:12-14

Blow the trumpet...gather the people...gather the children, even infants at the breast. Let the bridegroom leave his room, and the bride her canopy. ...let [them]...**weep**. Joel 2:15-17

Put on sackcloth and...**wail**.... **Sanctify a fast**, call a solemn assembly. Gather the elders and all the inhabitants of the land to the house of the Lord your God, and **cry out** to the Lord.... Joel 1:13,14

Indeed I heard _____[*your name*] pleading: "You disciplined me, and I took the discipline; I was like a calf untrained. Bring me back, let me come back, for You are the Lord my God. For after I had turned away **I repented**.... I was ashamed, and I was dismayed...." Therefore I am deeply moved for him; I will surely have mercy on him, says the Lord.
Jer. 31:18-20

And the people believed God; they proclaimed a fast, and everyone, great and small put on sackcloth. When the news reached the king, he rose from his throne, removed his robe, covered himself with sackcloth, and sat in ashes. Then he had a proclamation made..., "No human being or animal, no herd or flock shall taste anything. They shall not feed, nor shall they drink water. Human beings and animals shall be covered with sackcloth, and they shall *cry mightily* to God. All shall turn from their evil ways and from the violence that is in their hands. Who knows? God may relent and change His mind; He may turn from His fierce anger so that we do not perish." Jonah 3:5-9

At the evening sacrifice I got up from my fasting, with my garments and my mantle torn, and fell on my knees, spread out my hands to the Lord my God, and said, "O my God, I am too ashamed and embarrassed to lift my face to You, my God, for our iniquities have risen higher than our head, and our guilt has mounted up to the heavens...for we have forsaken Your commandments...." While Ezra prayed and **made confession, weeping** and throwing himself down before the house of God, a very great assembly of men, women, and children gathered to him out of Israel; the people also **wept bitterly**. Ezek. 9:5-6,10; 10:1

God's heart is towards all people, and He loves to forgive.

He does not retain anger forever because He delights in showing [mercy].
Micah 7:18

And should I [the Lord] not be concerned about Nineveh, that great city in which there are more than a 120 thousand persons who do not know their right hand from their left and also many animals? Jonah 4:11

When God saw what they did, how they turned from their evil ways, God changed His mind about the calamity that He had said He would bring upon them; and He did not do it. Jonah 3:10

{God even forgives Sodom.} I will restore their fortunes, the fortunes of Sodom and her daughters and the fortunes of Samaria and her daughters, and I will restore your own fortunes along with theirs. Ezek. 16:53

{God to Moses declaring His Name.} The Lord, the Lord, a God **merciful** and gracious, slow to anger, and abounding in steadfast Love and faithfulness, keeping steadfast Love for the thousandth generation, **forgiving** iniquity and transgression and sin. Ex. 34:6-7

The Lord is slow to anger but great in power. Nahum 1:3

At one moment I may declare concerning a nation or a kingdom, that I will pluck up and break down and destroy it, but if that nation, concerning which I have spoken, turns from its evil, I will change My mind about the disaster that I intended to bring on it. Jer. 18:7-8

Jonah...became angry..., "O Lord! Is not this...why I fled to Tarshish...; for I knew that You are a gracious God and **merciful**, slow to anger, and abounding in steadfast Love, and **ready to relent** from punishing." Jonah 4:2

{In fact, for one nation who wouldn't repent God cried.} I wail for Moab...I cry out...for the people.... I weep for you...! My heart moans like a flute.... Jer. 48:31-32,36

Thus says the Lord: Look, I am a potter shaping evil against you and devising a plan against you. Turn now, all of you from your evil way, and amend your ways and your doings. Jer. 18:11

Repent therefore, and turn to God so that your sins may be wiped out, so that times of refreshing may come from the presence of the Lord. Acts 3:19-20

He [God] sent Him [Jesus] first to you, to bless you by turning each of you from your wicked ways. Acts 3:26

If My people would but listen to Me...and would follow Me how quickly would I subdue their enemies and turn My hand against their foes! Ps. 81:13-14

This is and has always been God's plan and purpose—that all people would repent and turn to Him, listen to Him, and follow Him—so He can bless us and subdue our enemies. *And* so His Name will be known throughout the earth.

I have raised you up for the very purpose of showing My Power in you, so that My Name may be proclaimed in all the earth. Rom. 9:16

The plans of the Lord stand firm forever, the purposes of His heart through all generations. Ps. 33:11 NIV

(I hope you can find more verses to put here.)

Prayer about God's Ultimate Purpose

O Father, I thank You so much that You want all people to turn to You. Thank You that You are merciful and slow to anger. Thank You that You were patient with me, that You waited for me to come to repentance. May Your purpose be accomplished, Father. May Your will be done! By the power of the Blood of Yeshua HaMashiach, I pray the enemy will be defeated and banished from the earth, and cast into the lake of fire, so all people will turn to You. So Your perfect will and final, awesome plan can come to the universe. You have spoken, Adonai. Let Your Word accomplish the purpose for which You sent it!

(Go ahead and write a prayer here.)

Contend for the faith. Jude 3

Prophecies Against
Pride and Arrogance

Whenever I read through this section, I tremble to see how much God hates pride. May God help us keep every last trace of it out of our lives! Let's do warfare with these prophecies and pray for repentance from pride

For people to be shaken out of the stronghold of pride it sometimes takes a disaster that puts them in a situation where they are not in control anymore, . That is what it took for me. And that's the reason for these prophecies. Remember from the last section that God takes no pleasure in any of this. However, He loves His people too much to leave them lost in their doomed state of pride. I'm glad He didn't leave me there. I will thank Him always for the tragic event it took for me to begin to be shaken from my pride.

Why does God consider pride so wicked? It's because pride leads us toward rebellion and keeps us from turning to God. Rebellion is open rejection of God and thus an open invitation for the devil and his demons to come in. Rebellion leads to the most depraved state of man—being completely cut off from God.

So, let's repent of every last tinge of rebellion of any kind toward anyone in our lives, and then let's repent as Daniel, Nehemiah, and Ezra did for all the rebellion in America—especially ever since the sixties. Actually one could say this country's revolution was based on a seed of rebellion. So, let's repent for that germ of what we've been calling "independence" that has been in our culture from the very beginning. It sprouted its ugliness in the Civil War, with brother rebelling against brother, and is now coming to full fruit in these last five decades.

God comes in the storm of judgment to show His mighty powerful presence so people will repent in humility. The only entity God wants to "burn…to stubble" is the devil and his demons, and those who sell themselves to be their tools (people who are so full of pride they refuse to repent ever, such as the Pharaoh of Egypt and his army). It is all for the Glory of the Lord—that He be lifted up. We are not praying for the destruction of people, but of pride, and of satan and all his dark hosts.

Perhaps God gives us these prophecies and begins to bring the punishment upon us to spur His intercessors to intercede for the hearts of His people. Scripture says that sometimes the destruction comes because no one is interceding. (See pages 134-135)

I am against you, O arrogant one, says the Lord God of hosts; for your day has come, the time when I will punish you. The arrogant one shall stumble and fall, with no one to raise him up, and I will kindle a fire in his cities and it will devour everything around him.
Jer. 50:31-32

The Lord alone shall be exalted in that day. For the Lord of hosts has a day
Against all that is proud and lofty,
Against all that is lifted up and high.
Against all the cedars of Lebanon, lofty and lifted up;
And against all the oaks of Bashan;
Against all the high mountains
And against all the lofty hills;
Against every high tower,
And against every fortified wall;
Against all the ships of Tarshish,
And against all the beautiful craft.
The haughtiness of people shall be humbled,
And the pride of everyone shall be brought low;
And the LORD alone will be exalted on that day.
Is. 2:11-21

On that day people will throw away…their idols…to enter the caverns of the rocks and the clefts in the crags, from the terror of the LORD and from the Glory of His Majesty when He rises to terrify the earth. Is. 2:20-21

The high places…shall be destroyed. They shall say to the mountains, Cover us, and to the hills, Fall on us. Hos. 10:8

…on the day of the great slaughter when the towers fall. Is 30:25 (Our 9-11?)

Then…everyone…hid in the caves and among the rocks of the mountains, calling to the mountains and rocks, "Fall on us and hide us from the face of the one seated on the throne and from the wrath of the Lamb; for the great day of their wrath has come, and who is able to stand? Rev. 6:15-16

And the trees of the field shall know that I am the Lord.
I bring low the high tree.
I make high the low tree.
I dry up the green tree
And make the dry tree flourish.
I the Lord have spoken. I will accomplish. Ezek. 17:24

All who exalt themselves will be humbled. Lk. 18:14

People are bowed down, everyone is brought low, and the eyes of the haughty are humbled. But the Lord of hosts is exalted. Is. 5:5-6

The Lord of hosts has planned it—to defile the pride of all glory, to shame all the honored of the earth. Is. 23:9

For a long time I have held my peace, I have kept still and restrained myself; now I will cry out…. I will lay waste mountains and hills, and dry up all their herbage; I will turn the rivers into islands, and dry up the pools…. They shall be turned back and utterly put to shame—those who trust in carved images…. Is. 42:14-15,17

If you will not listen, if you will not lay it to heart to give glory to My Name, says the Lord of hosts, then I will send the curse on you and I will curse your blessings…and I will put you out of My presence. Mal. 2:1-2,3

I will punish the world for its evil, and the wicked for their iniquity; I will put an end to the pride of the arrogant, and lay low the insolence of tyrants. Is. 13:11

Because you have raged against Me and your arrogance has come to My ears, I will put My hook in your nose and My bit in your mouth; I will turn you back on the way by which you came. Is. 37:29

All those who are arrogant are an abomination to the Lord. Prov. 16:5

The Lord tears down the house of the proud. Prov. 15:25

See, the day is coming, burning like an oven, when all the arrogant and all evildoers will be stubble; the day that comes shall burn them up, says the Lord of hosts, so that it will leave them neither root nor branch. Mal. 4:1

The Mighty One has done great things.... He has shown strength with His arm; He has scattered the proud in their thoughts of their hearts. He has brought down the powerful from their thrones, and lifted up the lowly. Lk. 1:49,51-52 (Mary's prophecy)

Now I, Nebuchadnezzar, praise and extol and honor the King of heaven, for all His works are truth, and His ways are justice; and He is able to bring low those who walk in pride.
Dan. 4:37

(Yes, you are welcome to add verses about pride here.)

Prayer about Pride

Remember this, O Lord, how...an impious people reviles Your Name. Ps. 74:18

O Adonai Elohim, I wage prayer warfare against all the pride of the earth. In Your Name, I prophesy with Your Word against all strongholds of pride, that they will come tumbling down and will be crushed under our feet; that they will be swept away from the earth. I pray, Lord, that the peoples of the earth will not hide in the rocks, but rather will allow You to humble them with Your Holy Love. I pray that all hearts will come trembling, humbly out of their strongholds of pride and bow down in reverence to You; giving all glory and honor to You, their Father, and Yeshua, their Savior, the Lamb who was slain for them.

O Yeshua Adonai, deliver people from their pride. And remove all traces of rebellion from this generation. Do whatever it takes, Adonai, to cause everyone's spiritual towers of pride to come crashing down around their feet. So people can be set free and come to know You and Your Love and Your ways. So there will no longer be a people anywhere who reviles Your Name.

(Please add your prayers to help in this war against pride).

Pray without ceasing. I Thessalonians 5:17

The Judgment Storm
of the Lord
Against Rebellion
and Wickedness

Some of the following prophecies sound like what has been happening the last several years with the tsunami, hurricanes, earthquakes, tornadoes, etc. Perhaps they are already being fulfilled right before our eyes. Pray that people bow their knees in humble repentance to God that we may have God's mercy instead of judgment.

Look, the storm of the Lord! Wrath has gone forth, a whirling tempest [KJV: a grievous whirlwind]; it will burst upon the head of the wicked. The anger of the Lord will not turn back until He has executed and accomplished the intents of His mind. In the latter days you will understand it clearly. Jer. 23:19-20

The Lord is slow to anger but great in power, and the Lord will by no means clear the guilty. His way is in the whirlwind and the storm.... Nahum 1:3

See, the Lord has One who is mighty and strong like a hail storm, a destroying tempest, like a storm of mighty overflowing water; with His hand He will hurl them down to earth. Is. 28:2

"Look! Disaster is spreading from nation to nation; a mighty storm is rising from the ends of the earth." Jer. 25:32 NIV

You felt secure in your wickedness; you said, "No one sees me." ...But evil shall come upon you, which you cannot charm away; disaster shall fall upon you, which you will not be able to ward off; and ruin shall come on you suddenly. Is. 48:10,11

See, the Lord commands, and the great house shall be shattered to bits, and the little house to pieces. Amos 6:11

The city of chaos is broken down, every house is shut up so no one can enter. Is. 24:10

For the palace will be forsaken, the populous city deserted. Is. 32:14

Does disaster befall a city unless the Lord has done it? Amos 3:6

On the day I punish _____ [America!] for its transgressions...I will tear down the winter house as well as the summer house; and the houses of ivory shall perish, and the great houses shall come to an end, says the Lord. Amos 3:13,15

The Lord of hosts has sworn in my hearing: Surely many houses shall be desolate, large and beautiful houses, without inhabitant. Is. 5:9

Hail will sweep away the refuge of lies, and waters will overwhelm the shelter...when the overwhelming scourge passes through, you will be beaten down by it. Is. 28:17-18

In pride and arrogance of heart they said: "The bricks have fallen, but we will build with dressed stones; the sycamores have been cut down, but we will put cedars in their place." ... For all this His anger has not turned away; His hand is stretched out still. Is. 9:9-10,12

[They] may say, "Though we have been crushed, we will rebuild the ruins." But this is what the Lord Almighty says: "They may build, but I will demolish. They shall be called the Wicked Land, a people always under the wrath of the Lord. Mal. 1:4

For you have made the city a heap, the fortified city a ruin; the palace of aliens is a city no more, it will never be rebuilt.... Is. 25:2

Hear this Word, you cows of Bashan...who oppress the poor, who crush the needy, who say to their husbands, "Bring something to drink!" The Lord God has sworn by His holiness; the time is surely coming upon you, when they shall take you away with hooks, even the last of you with fishhooks. Through breaches in the wall you shall leave, each one straight ahead...says the Lord. Amos 4:1

No longer do they drink wine with singing. Strong drink is bitter to those who drink it. ...There is an outcry in the streets for lack of wine. Is. 24:9,11

They are a rebellious people, faithless children, children who will not hear the instruction of the Lord.... Therefore, thus says the Holy One of Israel: Because you reject this Word…therefore this iniquity shall become for you like a break in a high wall, bulging out, and about to collapse, whose crash comes suddenly, in an instant; its breaking is like that of a potter's vessel that is smashed. Is. 30:8,12-14

A thousand shall flee at the threat of one, at the threat of five you shall flee. Is. 30:17 {Could this maybe mean the category levels of hurricanes? When the level got to five everyone fled!}

The river gates are opened, the palace trembles. It is decreed that the city be exiled, …led away, moaning like doves and beating their breasts…like a pool whose waters run away…. Devastation, desolation, and destruction! Hearts faint and knees tremble, all loins quake, all faces grow pale! Nahum 2:6-10

There will be …distress among the nations confused by the roaring of the sea and the waves. People will faint from fear and foreboding of what is coming upon the world. Lk. 21:25-26

And in an instant, suddenly, you will be visited by the Lord of hosts with thunder and earthquake and great noise, with whirlwind and tempest, and the flame of a devouring fire. Is. 29:5-6

For I am the Lord your God, who stirs up the sea so that its waves roar…. Is. 51:15

Hear and give ear; do not be haughty, for the Lord has spoken. Give glory to the Lord your God before He brings darkness, and before your feet stumble on the mountains at twilight; while you look for light, He turns it into gloom and makes it deep darkness. Is. 13:15-16

O my poor people put on sackcloth, and roll in ashes; make mourning as for an only child, most bitter lamentation: for suddenly the destroyer will come upon us. Jer. 6:26

"Come out of her, My people! Run for your lives! Run from the fierce anger of the Lord." Jer. 51:45 NIV

The Lord protects those who turn to Him:

Come out of her, My people, so that you do not take part in her sins, and so that you do not share in her plagues; for her sins are heaped high as heaven, and God has remembered her iniquities. Rev. 18:4-5

…[C]all a solemn assembly; gather the people…; gather the children, even infants…. Let the bridegroom leave his room, and the bride her canopy…. Let them say, "Spare your people, O Lord…." Joel 2:15-17

The Lord is good, a stronghold in a day of trouble; He protects those who take refuge in Him, even in a rushing flood. Nahum 1:7-8 (Remember the orphans who were saved in the Tsunami in 2004!)

The Lord loves the righteous. The Lord watches over the strangers; He upholds the orphan and the widow, but the way of the wicked He brings to ruin. Ps. 146:8-9

When the tempest passes, the wicked are no more, but the righteous are established forever. Prov. 10:25

Those who listen to Me will be secure and will live at ease, without dread of disaster. Prov. 1:33

The Lord is exalted, He dwells on high; …He will be the stability of your times. Is. 33:6 (Another verse about God's protection would go nicely here.)

Prayers about the Storm of the Lord

Sept. 29, '05

Look, the storm of the Lord! Wrath has gone forth, a whirling tempest [kjv: a grievous whirlwind]; it will burst upon the head of the wicked. The anger of the Lord will not turn back until He has executed and accomplished the intents of His mind. [!!] In the latter days you will understand it clearly. [!!] Jer. 23:19-20

O Jesus we wage warfare with your prophetic Words. I pray your anger will NOT turn back until You have executed and accomplished the intents of Your mind. Let Your storm go forth. Let Your whirlwind come upon the head of the wicked until they turn from their wicked ways and turn to You, JESUS.

Sept. 22, '05

O Father, I pray, do whatever it takes to bring this country to its knees to stay on its knees in repentance to You. Please, Father, turn this nation back to You. Do whatever it takes to turn this country in meekness to You—everyone from the top to the bottom. May all cry out to you and repent on humble knees—knees that will stay bent!!

Oct. 12, '05

Monday, October 3 was the first day of Rosh Hoshana, the Feast of the Trumpets, this year. [It was also the day Kailey (my niece) died] Then on Saturday, October 8, there was a huge earthquake in Islamabad, Pakistan that affected Afghanistan and India also. It's all in Islamic territory. They are now saying 58,000 are dead! It's in the mountains of Kashmere, maybe where Osama Bin Laden is hiding. I haven't heard yet. Thursday, tomorrow, October 13, is Yom Kippur, the Day of Atonement. This is also the month of Ramadan. So it is a coinciding of Jewish and Muslim holidays, which happens very rarely! It is also a Hindu holiday I heard.

Jesus, I know this is not just coincidence. I know it is in Your plans somehow. While I'm mourning and praying for the victims (and wishing I could go help them), I'm wondering, are You coming back? Please come, Jesus, and rescue the people and rule on this earth.

March 23, '06

O Heavenly Father, I pray the places where you bring the judgment of disaster will learn from Your judgment. Holy Spirit, open their eyes to see why they were judged. Convict them of their sins and their wicked ways. I pray they will learn what You are trying to teach them. Do not let them go back and rebuild just to go on living the same as they did before. Please, Yeshua, I especially pray for New Orleans. Please, I pray that people there will stop glorifying and celebrating immorality. Open their eyes to see the ugliness and repulsiveness of wickedness. Cause them to repent and to hunger and thirst for righteousness and holiness. Give them new hearts that will honor and glorify You.

(I'm sure you know what to do now. So I will leave you in peace.)

Will not God grant justice to His chosen ones who cry to Him day and night? Luke 18:7

The Lord Brings Judgment

Let the sea roar, and all that fills it; the world and those who live in it. Let the floods clap their hands; let the hills sing together for joy at the presence of the Lord, for He is coming to judge the earth. He will judge the world with righteousness, and the peoples with equity. Ps. 98:7-9

Let the heavens be glad, and let the earth rejoice; let the sea roar, and all that fills it; let the field exult, and everything in it. Then shall all the trees of the forest sing for joy before the Lord; for He is coming, for He is coming to judge the earth. He will judge the world with righteousness, and the peoples with His truth. Ps. 96:11-13

For true and righteous are His judgments. Rev. 19:2 KJV
The judgments of the LORD are true and righteous altogether. Ps. 19:9 KJV

You are righteous, O Lord, and Your judgments are right. Ps. 119:137
Lord God Almighty, true and righteous are Thy judgments. Rev. 16:7 KJV

...The afflictions that you are enduring. This is evidence of the righteous judgment of God, and is intended to make you worthy of the kingdom of God.... II Thess. 1:4-5

The Lord! His adversaries shall be shattered; The Most High will thunder in heaven. The Lord will judge the ends of the earth. I Sam. 2:10 (Hannah's prophecy)

Arise, O Lord, let not man triumph; let the nations be judged in Your presence. Strike them with terror, O Lord; let the nations know they are but men. Ps. 9:19-20 NIV

The Lord will roar from on high; He will thunder from His holy dwelling and roar mightily against His land. He will shout like those who tread the grapes, shout against all who live on the earth. The tumult will resound to the ends of the earth, for the Lord will bring charges against the nations. He will bring judgment on all mankind and put the wicked to the sword. Jer. 25:30-31 NIV

Thus says the Lord, ...This time I will send all My plagues upon you...so that you may know that there is no one like Me in all the earth. For by now I could have...struck you and your people...and you would have been cut off from the earth. But this is why I have let you live: to show you My Power and to make My Name resound through all the earth. Ex. 9:13-16

The Lord will cause His majestic voice to be heard...when He strikes with His rod. Is. 30:30,31

See, the Name of the Lord comes from far away, burning with His anger, and in thick rising smoke; His lips are full of indignation, and His tongue is like a devouring fire; His breath is like an overflowing stream that reaches up to the neck—to sift the nations with the sieve of destruction.... And the Lord will cause His majestic voice to be heard and the descending blow of His arm to be seen, in furious anger and a flame of devouring fire, with a cloudburst and tempest and hailstones. Is. 30:27-30

The Lord will come in fire, and His chariots like the whirlwind, to pay back His anger in fury, and His rebuke in flames of fire. For by fire will the Lord execute judgment, and by His sword, on all flesh. Is. 66:15-16

The Lord has made Himself known, He has executed judgment. Ps. 9:16

Why the Lord brings judgment:

For when Your judgments are in the earth, the inhabitants of the world learn righteousness. If favor is shown to the wicked, they do not learn righteousness...they deal perversely and do not see the majesty of the Lord. O Lord, Your hand is lifted up, but they do not see it. Let them see Your zeal for Your people, and be ashamed. Let the fire for Your adversaries consume them.... O Lord, in distress they sought You, they poured out a prayer when Your chastening was on them. Is. 26:9-11,16

So, if you are ever asking why God would bring such harsh judgment, this is why. It is in distress that people seek the Lord, not in good times. What good is it for us to be in peace and security, and for things to go well, if we are not walking with the Lord? We need to pray for whatever it takes to turn all people to Jesus.

When I fed them to the full, they committed adultery and trooped to the houses of prostitutes. They were well-fed lusty stallions, each neighing for his neighbor's wife. Shall I not punish them for these things? Says the Lord; and shall I not bring retribution on a nation such as this? Jer. 5:7-9

But this people has a stubborn and a rebellious heart.... They do not say in their hearts, "Let us fear the Lord our God." Shall I not punish them for these things? Says the Lord; and shall I not bring retribution on a nation such as this? Jer. 5:29

They commit iniquity and are too weary to repent.... Shall I not punish them for these things? Says the Lord; and shall I not bring retribution on a nation such as this?
Jer. 9:5,9

I will now refine and test them, for what else can I do with My sinful people? Jer. 9:7

You [God] have wrapped Yourself with anger and pursued us, killing without pity; You have wrapped Yourself with a cloud so no prayer gets through. You have made us filth and rubbish. Lam. 3:43-44

The Lord goes forth like a soldier, like a warrior He stirs up His fury; He cries out, He shouts aloud, He shows Himself mighty against His foes. Is. 42:13

For the Lord is enraged against the nations, and furious against all their hoards; He has doomed them, has given them over for slaughter. Is. 34:2

Some passages sound horrible, especially if you read on in them. Remember that God does not take pleasure in any of this. Let's pray for the repentance that God longs for (see chapter 8).

Gather together, ...O shameless nation, before you are driven away like the drifting chaff, before there comes upon you the fierce anger of the Lord, before there comes upon you the day of the Lord's wrath. Zeph. 2:1-2

Will you indeed go unpunished? You will not go unpunished, for I am calling down a sword upon all who live on the earth, declares the Lord Almighty. Jer. 25:29 NIV

I overthrew some of you as when God overthrew Sodom and Gomorrah, and you were like a brand snatched from the fire; yet you did not return to Me, says the Lord.
Amos 4:11

Does disaster befall a city unless the Lord has done it? Amos 3:6

You have struck them, but they refused to take correction. They have made their faces harder than rock; they have refused to turn back. Jer. 5:3

There is no god besides Me....For I lift up My hand to heaven, ...as I live forever, ...My hand takes hold on judgment; I will take vengeance on My adversaries, and will repay those who hate Me.... Praise, O heavens, His people, worship Him...for He will take vengeance. Deut. 32:39,40,41,43

I am the Lord, and there is no other. I form light and create darkness, I make weal [peace and happiness] and create war; I the Lord do all these things. Is. 45:6-7

See now that I, even I, am He, there is no god besides me. I kill and I make alive, I wound and I heal; and no one can deliver from My hand. Deut. 32:39

For He wounds, but He binds up. He strikes but His hands heal. Job 5:18

Come let us return to the Lord, for it is He who has torn us and He will heal us. He has struck down, and He will bind us up. After two days He will revive us. On the third day He will raise us up that we may live with Him. Hos. 6:1-2

The light of the sun will be sevenfold, like the light of seven days, on the day when the Lord binds up the injuries of His people and heals the wounds inflicted by His blow. Is. 30:26

It is time for the Lord to act, for Your Law has been broken. Ps. 119:126

Does He who disciplines nations not punish? Ps. 94:10 NIV

Seek the Lord, all you humble of the land, who do His commands; seek righteousness, seek humility; perhaps you may be hidden on the day of the Lord's wrath. Zeph. 2:3

Come, My people, enter your chambers and shut your doors behind you. Hide yourselves for awhile until wrath is past. For the Lord comes out from His place to punish the inhabitants of the earth for their iniquity. Is. 26:20-21

(One purpose for hiding would be to pray, pray, pray!)

When the tempest passes, the wicked are no more, but the righteous are established forever. Prov. 10:25

"The Son of Man will send His angels, and they will collect out of His Kingdom all causes of sin and all evildoers, and they will throw them into the furnace of fire where there will be weeping and gnashing of teeth, THEN the righteous shall shine like the sun in the Kingdom of their Father." Matt. 13:41-43

"Now is the judgment of this world; now the ruler of this world will be cast out." Jn. 12:28 NKJV

Prayer about Judgment

O Father God, You are righteous. Even Your anger and fury are holy and righteous. Almighty God, we are but dust in Your Mighty Presence. Yet You love us. You care for all the people of the earth. You want all to forsake their wicked ways and come to You to be clothed in the righteousness of the Blood of Yeshua HaMashiach.

You love us so much that You plan to cast out all evil from the universe so we can dwell with You in peace. O Lord of Lords and King of Kings, Your will be done! Come and judge between Your righteousness and our unrighteousness; between good and evil. Come to the earth in Your fury and banish all evil. Remove it and throw it into the Lake of Fire.

O Lord God, we glorify Your Holy judgment. Judge our hearts, Lord, and remove all sin from us. Cleanse us by the Blood of the Lamb. We thank You that we are safe from Your anger because of Yeshua's sacrifice. We thank You that we shall dwell with You where there will only be purity and holiness. O how we long for that day, Jesus/Yeshua! Bring Your judgment to remove all darkness. Let Your judgment come that it may hasten the day of total LIGHT.

Feb. 7, '06

Glenn (my husband) has been talking about the Holiness of God. He said, "God is Holy, Holy, Holy. His love is Holy and even His judgment is Holy." I agreed. I said that even His anger that the prophets talk about is Holy—even the wrath of fire coming out from His mouth is not contaminated like our anger is.

Glenn said that if we don't see how Holy God is then we don't understand the need for the Cross. I agreed and added that if we don't see how Holy God is, we also don't see how horribly sinful we are. He agreed. Then he noted that the angels and living creatures don't cry out about God's other attributes. "They don't say, 'Love, love, love.'" He said, "Our word 'love' doesn't begin to describe God. They don't say, 'Mercy, mercy, mercy.' They say, 'Holy, Holy, Holy.' I don't think we even *begin* to know how Holy God is." On and on he talked about God's Holiness. It was so wonderful!

Praise You, Yeshua Adonai. Please keep on revealing Your Holiness to us.

.

Pray in the Spirit at all times in every prayer and supplication.

Ephesians 6:18

We Bring the Lord's Judgment Upon Ourselves

You may think that God's judgment and punishment sound way too harsh, but these Scriptures show that we people bring it upon ourselves. We deserve it.

Have you not brought this upon yourself by forsaking the Lord your God while He led you in the way? Jer. 2:17

See, the Lord's hand is not too short to save, nor His ear too dull to hear. Rather, your iniquities have been barriers between you and your God, and your sins have hidden His face from you so that He does not hear. Is. 59:1-2

Your ways and your doings have brought this upon you. This is your doom; how bitter it is! Jer. 4:18

Who gave up ____[my city] to the spoiler, and ____ [my country] to the robbers? Was it not the Lord, against whom we have sinned, in whose ways [we] would not walk, and whose law [we] would not obey? Is. 42:24

What wrong did your ancestors find in Me that they went far from Me, and went after worthless things, and became worthless themselves? Jer. 2:4

For you forsake the Lord your God; the fear of Me is not in you, says the Lord God of hosts.... Why do you complain against Me? You have all rebelled against Me, says the Lord. Jer. 2:19,29

I will chastise you in just measure, and I will by no means leave you unpunished.... I have dealt you the blow of an enemy, the punishment of a merciless foe, because your guilt is great, because your sins are so numerous. Why do you cry out over your hurt? Your pain is incurable. Because your guilt is great, because your sins are so numerous, I have done these things to you. Jer. 30:11,14-15

For I have hidden My face from this city because of all their wickedness. Jer. 33:5

It [the destruction of a city] was for the sins of her prophets and the iniquities of her priests. Lam. 4:13

The people of the land have practiced extortion and committed robbery; they have oppressed the poor and needy, and have extorted from the alien without redress.... Therefore I have poured out My indignation upon them; I have consumed them with the fire of My wrath; I have returned their conduct upon their heads, says the Lord God. Ezek. 22:29,31

Listen, you...who hate the good and love the evil.... {Is that not America today?} They will cry to the Lord, but He will not answer them; He will hide His face from them at that time, because they have acted wickedly. Micah 3:1,2,3

I the Lord have spoken; the time is coming, I will act. I will not refrain, I will not spare, I will not relent. According to your ways and your doings I will judge you, says the Lord God.
Ezek. 24:14

I am weary of relenting.... Jer. 15:17

Thus says the Lord of hosts.... The **Word** of the Lord is to them an object of scorn; they take no pleasure in it. But I am full of the wrath of the Lord; I am weary of holding it in.
Jer. 6:9, 10-11

You shall know that I, the Lord, have heard all the abusive speech that you uttered.... And you magnified yourselves against Me with your mouth, and multiplied your words against Me; I heard it. Thus says the Lord God: As the whole earth rejoices, I will make you desolate.
Ezek. 35:12,13-14

I will stretch out My hand against...those who have turned back from following the Lord, who have not sought the Lord or inquired of Him. Zeph. 1:4,6

I will bring such distress upon people that they shall walk like the blind; because they have sinned against the Lord.... Neither their silver nor their gold will be able to save them on the day of the Lord's wrath. Zeph. 1:17,18

The wicked return to the grave, all the nations that forget God. Ps. 9:17 NIV

This was the guilt of your sister Sodom: she and her daughters had pride, excess of food, and prosperous ease, but did not aid the poor and needy. They were haughty, and did abominable things before Me; therefore I removed them when I saw it.... You have committed more abominations than they, and have made your sisters appear righteous by all the abominations that you have committed. Ezek. 16:49-50

Now the end is upon you. I will loose My anger upon you. I will judge you according to your ways, ...I will have no pity. I will punish you for your ways. Then you shall know that I am the Lord. Ezek. 7:3,4

So their root will become rotten.... For they have rejected the instruction of the Lord of hosts and have despised the Word of the Holy One. Is. 31:2

Woe to you who strive with their Maker. Is. 45:9
Do not scoff, or your bonds will be made stronger. Is. 28:22

The people did not turn to Him who struck them, or seek the Lord of hosts.... For all this His anger has not turned away, His hand is stretched out still. Is. 9:13,17

Though I say to the righteous that they shall surely live, yet if they trust in their righteousness and commit iniquity, none of their righteous deeds shall be remembered; but in the iniquity that they have committed they shall die. Ezek. 33:13

All day long I have held out My hands to a disobedient and contrary people.
Rom. 10:21

I held out My hands all day long to a rebellious people, who walk in a way that is not good, following their own devices [note: imaginations]; a people who provoke Me to My face continually. Is. 65:2-3

Turn now, all of you from your evil way.... But they say, "It is no use! We will follow our own plans." Jer. 18:11-12

The earlier prophets proclaimed: ...Turn from your evil ways and your evil practices. But they would not listen or pay attention to Me, declares the Lord. Zech. 1:4 NIV

They refused to pay attention; Stubbornly they turned their backs and stopped up their ears...and would not listen to the...Words that the Lord Almighty sent by His Spirit.
Zech. 7:11-12 NIV

The more I called them, the more they went from Me. Hos. 11:2

"When I called, they did not listen; so when they called, I would not listen," says the Lord Almighty. Zech. 7:13 NIV

Because I have called and you refused, have stretched out My hand and no one heeded, and because you have ignored all My counsel and would have none of My reproof, I also will laugh...when panic strikes you like a storm, and your calamity comes like a whirlwind, when distress and anguish come upon you. Then they will call upon Me, but I will not answer; they will seek Me diligently, but will not find Me. Prov. 1:24-28

I will destine you to the sword, and all of you shall bow down to the slaughter; because, when I called, you did not answer, when I spoke, you did not listen, but you did what was evil in My sight, and chose what I did not delight in...says the Lord God.

Is. 65:12-13

According to their deeds, so will He repay. Is. 59:18

I will not keep silent, but I will repay; I will indeed repay into their laps their iniquities..., says the Lord. Is. 65:6-7

I will turn your deeds back upon your own heads swiftly and speedily. Joel 3:4,7

I have returned their conduct upon their heads, says the Lord God. Ezek. 22:31

The wicked are snared in the work of their own hands. Ps. 9:16

Their mischief returns upon their own heads, and on their own heads their violence descends. Ps. 7:16

But they rebelled and grieved His Holy Spirit; therefore He became their enemy; He Himself fought against them. Is. 63:10

And they shall go out and look at the dead bodies of the people who have rebelled against Me; for their worm shall not die, their fire shall not be quenched, and they shall be an abhorrence to all flesh. Is. 66:24

Perhaps you are thinking, "But these are just Old Testament Scriptures. Jesus isn't that harsh!" You are wrong. Here are the words of Jesus.

"Whoever disobeys the Son will not see life, but must endure God's wrath."

Jn. 3:36

"Woe to you Chorazin...Bethsaida! For if the deeds of power done in you had been done in Tyre and Sidon, they would have repented.... And you, Capernaum, ...you will be brought to Hades" Lk. 10:13,15 (There is no town at Capernaum today, only some ruins and a museum.)

"...His Lord handed him over to be tortured.... So My Heavenly Father will also do to every one of you, if you do not forgive...from your heart." Matt. 18:34-35

"If...he begins to beat his fellow slaves and eats and drinks with drunkards, the Master...will cut him in pieces [note: cut him off] and put him with hypocrites, where there will be weeping and gnashing of teeth." Matt. 24:47-51

"'As for the worthless slave, throw him in outer darkness, where there will be weeping and gnashing of teeth.'" Matt. 25:30

"And these will go away into eternal punishment." Matt.25:46

"You snakes, you brood of vipers! How can you escape being sentenced to hell?"

Matt.24:33

"Beware of…hypocrisy. Nothing is covered up that will not be uncovered, and nothing secret that will not become known…. Whatever you have said in the dark will be heard… and what you have whispered behind closed doors will be proclaimed from the housetops."
Lk. 12:1-3

"But God said to him, 'You fool! This very night your life is being demanded of you….' So it is with those who store up treasures for themselves." Lk. 12:20-21

"Therefore none of you can become My disciple if you do not give up all your possessions." Lk. 15:33

"Everyone who falls on that stone will be broken to pieces, and it will crush anyone on whom it falls." Lk. 20:18

"Whoever does not abide in Me is thrown away…into the fire and burned. Jn. 15:6

"Every tree that does not bear good fruit is cut down and thrown into the fire."
Lk. 3:9

"For those who do not have, even what they seem to have will be taken away."
Lk. 8:18

"Unless you repent, you will all perish." Lk. 13:15

Other New Testament Scriptures and more Old Testament ones:

Moses said, "The Lord your God will raise up for you from your own people a prophet like me…. And it will be that everyone who does not listen to that prophet will be utterly rooted out of the people." Acts 4:22,23

Judgment will be without mercy to anyone who has shown no mercy. James 2:13

They refused to love the truth and so be saved. …all who have not believed the truth but took pleasure in unrighteousness will be condemned. II Thess. 2:11-12

Because of these things [fornication, impurity, greed, obscene, silly, and vulgar talk, etc.] the wrath of God comes on those who are disobedient. Eph. 5:6

Let marriage be held in honor by all…for God will judge fornicators and adulterers.
Heb. 13:4

The Lord knows how to…keep the unrighteous under punishment…—especially those who indulge their flesh…, and who despise authority. II Pet. 2:9-10

Their end is destruction. Phil. 3:19

…they…will be destroyed, suffering the penalty for doing wrong. II Pet. 2:12-13

Their condemnation…has not been idle, and their destruction is not asleep.
II Pet. 2:3

For if, after they have escaped the defilements of the world through…Jesus…, they are again entangled in them and overpowered, the last state has become worse for them than the first. II Pet. 2:20

For it is impossible to restore again to repentance those who have once been enlightened, and have tasted the heavenly gift, and have shared in the Holy Spirit, and have tasted the goodness of the Word of God and the powers of the age to come, and then have fallen away, since on their own they are crucifying again the Son of God and are holding Him up to contempt. Heb. 6:4-6

America had better heed this warning today!

Do not defile yourselves in any of these ways, for by all these practices [adultery, incest, sacrificing babies or children (like abortion today), homosexual acts, and bestiality]...the land became defiled; and I punished it for its iniquity and the land vomited out its inhabitants... otherwise the land will vomit you out for defiling it, as it vomited out the nation that was before you. Lev. 18:24-25,28

All who hear the Words...and bless themselves, thinking in their hearts, "We are safe even though we go our own stubborn ways," ...the Lord's anger and passion will smoke against them. All the curses written in this Book will descend on them, and the Lord will blot out their names from under heaven. The Lord will single them out...for calamity, in accordance with all the curses...in this Book of Law. Deut. 29:19-21

They...would not listen to the Law or the Words that the Lord Almighty had sent by His Spirit.... So the Lord Almighty was very angry.... "I scattered them with a whirlwind among all the nations, where they were strangers. The land was left so desolate behind them that no one could come or go." Zech. 7:10-11 NIV

When you see their ways and their deeds, you will be consoled...and you shall know that it was not without cause that I did all that I have done..., says the Lord God.
                                                                                                Ezek. 14:22,23

For it is indeed just of God to repay with affliction those who afflict you, and to give relief to the afflicted...when Jesus is revealed from heaven with His mighty angels in flaming fire, inflicting vengeance on those who do not know God and on those who do not obey the Gospel of our Lord Jesus.... II Thess. 1:6-8

Repent and turn from all your transgressions; otherwise iniquity will be your ruin. Cast away from you all the transgressions that you have committed against Me and get yourselves a new heart and a new spirit! Why will you die...? Ezek. 18:30-31

What will save us from God's judgment which we have brought upon ourselves? Repentance and turning to His Son, Jesus. Reading all these Scriptures makes me tremble with thankfulness for God's mercy in sending us Jesus to take our punishment for our sins. Let's pray that the whole world comes to true repentance.

Here is true repentance:

In all that has happened to us, You have been just; You have acted faithfully, while we did wrong. Neh. 9:33 NIV

Our leaders...did not follow Your law, they did not pay attention to Your commands or the warnings You gave them. Neh. 9:34

For our transgressions before You are many, and our sins testify against us. Our transgressions indeed are with us, and we know our iniquities: transgressing, and denying the Lord, and turning away from following our God. Is. 59:12-13

Just as it is written in the law of Moses, all this calamity has come upon us. We did not entreat the favor of the Lord our God, turning from our iniquities and reflecting on His fidelity. So the Lord kept watch over this calamity until He brought it upon us. Indeed, the Lord our God is right in all that He has done; for we have disobeyed His voice.

Dan. 9:13-14

"O my God, I am too ashamed and embarrassed to lift my face to You, my God, for our iniquities have risen higher than our head, and our guilt has mounted up to the heavens...for we have forsaken Your commandments.... After all that has come upon us for our evil deeds and for our great guilt, seeing that You, our God, have punished us less than our iniquities deserved...shall we break your commandments again...? Would You not be angry with us until You destroy us without remnant or survivor? O Lord, God of Israel, You are just." Ezra 9: 6,10,13-15

"Then they repented and said, 'The Lord Almighty has done to us what our ways and practices deserve.'" Zech. 1:6

Let us test and examine our ways, and return to the Lord. Let us lift up our hearts as well as our hands to God in heaven. Lam. 3:40-41

The Lord is in the right, for I have rebelled against His Word. Lam. 1:18

I must bear the indignation of the Lord, because I have sinned against Him.

Micah 7:9

"'God, be merciful to me, a sinner!'" Lk. 18:13

Prayer about Judgment We Bring Upon Ourselves

O Lord God Almighty, ALL powerful and ALL holy, we bow, trembling before You, for our sins are so many they reach the heavens. We have rebelled against You and Your Word. We deserve every punishment You send us.

But thank You that we can approach You under the Blood of Yeshua HaMashiach. O Father, we plead the Blood. We repent in sackcloth and ashes. Forgive us for our sins. Forgive our nation! Forgive the world! O Father, bring us all to repentance.

Thank You, Lord/Adonai, that You do not let us rest in our sin and rebellion. Thank You that You do not let us remain apart from You. Thank You that You bring disaster and judgment so we can be shaken out of our reverie and wallowing and can turn from our own ways and follow You. Judge us, Lord. Judge the earth. Do whatever it takes. Do whatever You need to do to turn all hearts toward You!

Lord, we fight with You. May You win! May all evil be banished. May all people come to worship You. May the enemy get NO ONE!!! Hallelujah! Amen!

May 16, '06

Jesus told them a parable about their need to pray always and not to lose heart. "...There was a widow who kept coming...and saying, 'Grant me justice against my opponent.'...Will not God grant justice to His chosen ones who cry to Him day and night? Will He delay long in helping them: I tell you, He will quickly grant justice to them." Lk. 18:1,3,7-8

O Jesus/Yeshua, we must cry to You day and night. Help us not to lose heart. Help us to keep crying out to You day and night for Your justice against our opponent, the enemy—for freedom from him—for him to be completely DESTROYED! Grant us justice, Yeshua!! Do not delay. Come quickly and banish evil from the earth!

So that through death He might destroy the one who has the power of death, that is, the devil.... Heb. 2:14

O Yeshua, You came to destroy the devil—to *destroy* him. O Lord Jesus, Yeshua Adonai, may he be destroyed!! Destroy him and his power of death! May he be completely and utterly destroyed forever and ever!!! By the power of Your Holy Name. Amen!

Dec. 3, '03

Go now...inscribe it in a book so it may be for the time to come as a witness forever. For they are a rebellious people...who will not hear the instruction of the Lord.... Therefore thus says the Holy One of Israel: Because you reject this Word...iniquity shall become for you like a break in a high wall...bulging...collapse...crash...smashed.... ...in returning and rest you shall be saved... in quietness and trust your strength. But you refused.... "No, we will flee." ...His breath is like an overflowing stream that reaches up to the neck to sift the nations with the sieve of destruction, and to place on the jaws of the peoples a bridle that leads them astray (Is. 30:8,12,15,28). (!!!!) So it's not the enemy! It's the Lord!!! He's doing it as a punishment for unbelief—for rejection of His Word (v. 12)—for refusing to return to rest and quietness to be saved (v. 15)—for trusting in horses and chariots (Is. 31:1) instead of God!

So, I need to trust You, Lord, even in the awful things today like the deceit of children through the Harry Potter books, etc. You are doing it and You are in control!!!

I've been wrong in assuming I have to pray hard to get You, God, to notice the evil and do something about it!! Bing bing! I've thought that You were like the kind of parents who just let their kids be naughty and decide to ignore it. But if You seem like that, You are doing it *on purpose* for a good reason. You're doing it out of mercy for Your people, to give them time and many chances to come to You and listen to You. It's so nice to realize anew, Lord, that You are also upset that people of the world are "rebellious" and "faithless" and "won't hear Your instruction."

But...the Lord will cause His majestic voice to be heard...when He strikes with His rod.

Is. 30:30,31

And now I must trust You even if it seems like You are waiting too long and punishing the offspring instead of the real culprits. I must not judge or jump to conclusions. My perception is wrong. I must TRUST YOU, GOD!!!

Help me, Jesus, to trust You more and more. Help me to "return and rest" "in quietness and trust" so I shall be saved and find strength.

Mar. 22, '06

O Lord, may all the people of the earth learn from Your judgments. May they all return to You in quietness and trust. Rescue the children, Yeshua. Rescue them from being led astray and deceived. Protect them, Yeshua, and bring them to the Light of Your Truth.

O Jesus/Yeshua, You hate the sin of witchcraft. It is an abomination to You. Yet even Christian parents are blinded to the evil dangers of the Harry Potter books. Open their eyes to see, Jesus. Show them in Your Word.

You shall not suffer a witch [wiccan] *to live.* Ex. 22:18

When you enter the land the Lord your God is giving you, do not learn to imitate the detestable ways of the nations there. Let no one be found among you who sacrifices his son or daughter in the fire, who practices divination or sorcery, interprets omens, engages in witchcraft, or casts spells, or who is a medium or spiritist or who consults the dead. Anyone who does these things is detestable to the Lord, and because of these detestable practices the Lord your God will drive out those nations before you. You must be blameless before the Lord your God. Deut. 18:9-13 NIV

I will cut off witchcraft. Micah 5:12 KJV

The acts of the sinful nature are obvious: sexual immorality; ...idolatry and witchcraft; [NRSV: *sorcery*]...*drunkenness, orgies,* [NRSV: *carousing*] *and the like.* NRSV: *I am warning you, as I warned you before: those who do such things will not inherit the kingdom of God.* Gal. 5:20-21 NIV then NRSV

Abstain from all appearance of evil. I Thess. 5:22 KJV

Jesus, why do parents want their children to be exposed to anything that even resembles evil? Give the parents hearts of compassion that are careful to protect their children from anything that is not of You.

O Yeshua Adonai, don't let us lose a whole generation of children. In Your Name, Yeshua HaMashiach, I rebuke the deceit and witchcraft of the Harry Potter books and movies. I silence the falsehood and blasphemy that raises itself up against God. I demolish it all in the Holy, Powerful Name of Jesus. I speak to it to be removed and cast into the Lake of Fire. Never to deceive any children again. Never to turn any child away from the Lord again. In Your Holy Name, JESUS/ YESHUA. Let it Be! Amen, Hallelujah!!

Nov. 30, '05

Jesus, in Your Name, I bind in chains the evil spirit of Harry Potter witchcraft. I crush that spirit by the power of the Blood. I banish it from the earth. I speak to it to be removed and cast into the fiery furnace. Be removed from the theaters. Be removed from the video stores, from the internet, and from bookstores. Be removed from all homes. Be removed from TV. Be removed from all churches. Be removed from all children's minds and emotions and hearts and memories. I declare that its power is broken—defeated on the Cross. Its attraction is broken and ruined; its influence annihilated and wiped out in the Holy Name of Jesus Christ of Nazareth

April 26, '04

Haley's Bible Handbook (Henry H. Haley, Twenty-Fourth Edition, Zondervan Publishing House, Grand Rapids, MI, 1965), on pages 166 and 198 tells about excavation items found in 1904-1909 that reveal the evils of the Canaanites: jars of baby bones, cemeteries of newborn babies. They sacrificed their firstborns. They built a child into a wall of their houses for good luck on the whole family. They had idols with exaggerated sex organs, and had male and female prostitute priests. They worshiped with fornication and then sacrificed the resultant babies.

Here's a quote from p. 167 "Do we wonder any longer why God commanded...to exterminate the Canaanites? Did a civilization of such abominable filth and brutality have any right [any] longer to exist?"

But, Lord, it is our society today! We have bones of aborted babies. And lots of them would be firstborn! Our TV and movies are full of fornication. People's *lives* are full of fornication. Many Christians think nothing of watching it on the screen, helping to fund it! And our pornography business rakes in huge profits!

Our fashions for decades have been exaggerating the sensual curves of the body, and exposing the bare skin of those curves. We've even been proud of looking sexy! We worship the body and sex and so-called "sexual freedom." We march in Washington D.C. in the 100's of thousands in support of killing our babies and having "sexual freedom." Hiliary Clinton said at a pro-abortion march in D.C. that abortion has to do with "...faith." (!!!!) I saw a grandmother with her young granddaughters proudly marching for their "freedom" to someday abort their babies! Her darling sweet, innocent granddaughters!! One was still in a stroller!! I was aghast!

The writer of *Haley's Commentary* in 1927 (first edition) could not have imagined our own culture getting this bad!!! Never could he have imagined in a million years it would turn out like this!!

O Lord Jesus, I repent for our country! Our sins are so many they do reach to the very heavens. O Jesus, bring us to repentance!

April 28, '04

Jesus, you destroyed the Canaanites for having a culture as bad as ours. Is our destruction near? Are there enough righteous people in USA to spare the country? (There weren't enough in Sodom and Gomorrah or in Canaan.) Is Your coming near, Jesus? Come Lord Jesus, COME QUICKLY!! Your Bride is waiting for you.

Only by prayer and fasting. Mark 9:29 NJKV

The Lord's Righteous Army Bringing His Judgment

Pray that we repent and allow God to cleanse us with Jesus' blood and sanctify us, so we can be used by Him for His righteous judgment.

Let the one who has My Word speak My Word faithfully.... Is not My Word like fire, says the Lord, and like a hammer that breaks a rock in pieces? Jer. 23:28,29

For the Lord takes pleasure in His people; He adorns the **humble** with victory. Let the **faithfu**l exult in glory.... Let the high praises of God be in their throats and two-edged swords [God's Word] in their hands, to execute vengeance on the nations and punishment on the peoples, to bind their kings with fetters and their nobles with chains of iron, to execute on them the judgment decreed. This is glory for all **His faithful ones**. Praise the Lord! Ps. 149:4-9

But for **you who revere My Name** the Sun of Righteousness shall rise, with healing in its wings. You shall go out leaping like calves from the stall. And you shall tread down the wicked, for they will be ashes under the soles of your feet, on the day when I act, says the Lord of hosts. Mal. 4: 2-3

You are My war club, My weapon of battle: with you I smash nations; with you I destroy kingdoms. Jer. 51:20-21

Now, I will make of you a threshing sledge, sharp, new, and having teeth; you shall thresh the mountains and crush them, and you shall make the hills like chaff. You shall winnow them and the wind shall carry them away, and the tempest shall scatter them. Is. 41:15-16

The Lord utters his voice at the head of His army; how vast is His host! Numberless are those who obey His command. Truly the day of the Lord is great; terrible indeed. Joel 2:11

On a bare hill raise a signal, cry aloud to them; wave the hand for them to enter the gates of the nobles. I Myself have commanded **My consecrated ones**, have summoned My warriors, My proudly exulting ones, to execute My anger. Listen, a tumult on the mountains as of a great multitude! Listen, an uproar of kingdoms, of nations gathering together! The Lord of hosts is mustering an army for battle. Is. 13:2-4

Proclaim this among the nations: Prepare war, stir up the warriors. Let all the soldiers draw near, let them **come up** [the rapture?]. Beat your plowshares into swords and your pruning hooks into spears; [!!] let the weakling say, "I am a warrior." Come quickly, all you nations all around, gather yourselves and **come up** to the valley...for there I will sit to judge all the neighboring nations. Joel 3:9-12

Behold, the Lord comes with **His myriads of holy ones**—the thousands of **His saints** to execute judgment upon all. Jude 14 AMP [Prophesied by Enoch.]

And the armies of heaven, wearing fine linen, white and pure, were following Him on white horses.... From His mouth comes a sharp sword..... He will tread the wine press of the fury of the wrath of God the Almighty. Rev. 19:14,15

Then I saw the beast and the kings of the earth with their armies gathered to make war against the Rider on the horse and against His army. Rev. 19:19

(I am aware that some of this will occur after the rapture, but that doesn't mean it is no concern of ours. It is still very much our concern since we will be fighting with the Lord and judging with Him. We need to care about it as much as our Lord does. We need to care enough to start preparing ourselves and to start praying that it comes to pass.)

Prayer about the Lord Using the Righteous

O Yeshua Adonai, we are in awe that You want to use us, who are but dust, to fight with You. We bow to You in humble thankfulness. We are overwhelmed with gratitude. We want to fight with You! Thank You for giving us the will to want to. Help us. Teach us. Make us pure by Your Blood so we are worthy to fight with You. So that we do not hinder the fight, but are actually a benefit to it!

Let us begin now in spiritual warfare. Make us ready, Yeshua. Let us come out into battle with You and defeat the foe completely. Unite us in this battle plan, Jesus. Let us be of one heart against all evil.

Yeshua, together with You, we bind the enemy, and all his hosts, with fetters and chains. We execute Your judgment upon them. In Your Name and by Your Power and Authority, we banish them to the Lake of Fire. May Your people be free forever from this menace!! Amen, Hallelujah!!

Nov. 15, '04

In Revelation 19:14-15 the troops of heaven, in linen clean and white, fight with Jesus against evil. We won't be in that army until even our anger is pure, until we are only angry at what God and Jesus are angry at.

Lord, teach me how to have only Godly anger. Teach me how to fight righteously in Your army—to fight in unity and one with You—to judge only what You judge.

You wait 400 years for iniquity to be full. *Your offspring shall be...oppressed for **four hundred years**; but I will bring judgment on the nation that they serve...and they shall come back here in the fourth generation; for the iniquity of the Amorites is not yet complete* (Gen. 15:13-15). Give us understanding that we may wait with You, Lord.

Only those with linen pure and white will reign with You. But we must remove the moats from our eyes, and discard our filthy garments first. Make us pure and white, Jesus, by Your Blood. Then *we will tread the wicked as ashes under our feet* (Mal. 4:3).

Far be it from me that I should sin against the Lord by ceasing to pray for you. I Samuel 12:23

Prophecies about Trembling and Quaking

There are two kinds of trembling. There's the good kind: trembling in awe; and there's the bad kind: trembling in fear. We will all tremble one way or the other. Pray!

Every time I read this section it makes me tremble with awe at how infinitely vast and powerful God is. It makes me want to fall at His feet in new humility and worship. I often read it out loud to myself. I want God to shake me and my life. I want everything that is not from Him to be removed. I want the same for our beloved world. Let all that is not of God be shaken until it crumbles to pieces.

Bring it to pass, Jesus. Shake this world until all evil is gone and until all people tremble in worship to You.

But this is the one to whom I will look, to the humble and contrite in spirit, who **trembles** at My Word. Is. 66:2

Worship the Lord in Holy Splendor; **tremble** before Him all the earth. Ps. 96:9

The Lord is king; let the peoples **tremble**! He sits enthroned upon the cherubim; let the earth **quake**! Ps. 99:1

"Should you not fear Me?" declares the Lord. "Should you not **tremble** in My presence?" Jer. 5:22 NIV

Fire goes before Him and consumes His adversaries on every side. His lightnings light up the world; the earth sees and **trembles**. The mountains **melt** like wax before the Lord, before the Lord of all the earth. The heavens proclaim His righteousness; and all the peoples behold His glory. All worshippers of images are put to shame.... Ps. 96:3-7

Hear, you peoples, all of you; listen, O earth, and all that is in it.... For lo, the Lord is coming out of His place.... Then the mountains will **melt** under Him and the valleys will **burst open**, like wax near the fire, like waters poured down a steep place. All this is for the transgression of ____[your city] and for the sins of ____[your country]. Micah 1:2-5

For the windows of heaven are opened, and the foundations of the earth **tremble**, the earth is utterly **broken**...torn asunder.... The earth is violently **shaken**. Is. 24:18-19

See, the Lord is riding on a swift cloud and comes to _____. The idols of _____ will **tremble** at His presence, and the heart of the _____s will **melt** within them. Is. 19:1

Tremble, you women who are at ease, **shudder**, you complacent ones...put sackcloth on your loins.... Is. 32:11

Kings shall see and stand up, and princes, and they shall **prostrate** themselves because of the Lord, who is faithful. Is. 49:7

So He shall **startle** many nations; kings shall **shut their mouths** because of Him. Is. 52:15

The sinners...are afraid; **trembling** has seized the godless: "Who among us can live with the devouring fire...the everlasting flames?" Is. 33:14

They shall **tremble** every moment for their lives, each one of them. Ezek. 32:14 NIV

O that You would tear open the heavens and come down, so that the mountains would **quake** at Your presence.... To make Your Name known to Your adversaries, so that the nations might **tremble** at Your presence. Is. 64:1

I will establish My covenant with you and you shall know that I am the Lord in order that you may remember and be **confounded,** and **never** open your mouth again because of your shame, when I forgive you all that you have done, says the Lord. Ezek. 16:24

For in My jealousy and in My blazing wrath I declare: On that day there shall be a great **shaking** in the land of Israel...and all human beings that are on the face of the earth, shall **quake** at My Presence, and the mountains shall be **thrown down**, and the cliffs shall **fall**, and every wall shall **tumble** to the ground.... And I will pour down torrential rains and hailstones, fire and sulfur.... So I will display My greatness and My Holiness and make Myself known in the eyes of many nations. Then they shall know that I am the Lord.

Ezek. 38:19-23

Blow the trumpet in Zion; sound the alarm on My holy mountain! Let all the inhabitants of the land **tremble,** for the day of the Lord is coming, it is near. Joel 2:1

The earth **quakes** before them, the heavens **tremble.** Joel 2:10

The Lord roars from Zion, and utters His voice from Jerusalem, and the heavens and the earth **shake**. Joel 3:16

The voice of the Lord **breaks** [NIV: splinters] the cedars of Lebanon. The voice of the Lord flashes forth flames of fire. The voice of the Lord **shakes** the wilderness. The voice of the Lord causes oaks to **whirl** and **strips** the forest bare. And in His temple ALL say, "Glory!"

Ps. 29:5-9

The earth **reeled** and **rocked**, the foundations of the mountains **trembled** and **quaked**.... He rode on a cherub and...came swiftly on the wings of the wind.... Out of the brightness before Him there **broke** through His clouds hailstones and coals of fire. The Lord also **thundered** in the heavens and the Most High uttered His voice.... He flashed forth lightning.... Then the channels of the sea were seen and the foundations of the world were laid bare. Ps. 18:7,10,12-15

O God, when the waters saw You they were afraid; the very deep **trembled**.... The skies thundered; Your arrows flashed on every side. The crash of Your thunder was in the whirlwind; Your lightnings lit up the world; the earth **trembled** and **shook**. Ps. 77:16-18

I looked on the earth, and lo, it was waste and void; and to the heavens, and they had no light. I looked on the mountains, and lo, they were **quaking**, and all the **hills moved to and fro**. I looked, and lo, there was no one at all, and all the birds of the air had **fled**. I looked and lo, the fruitful land was a desert, and all its cities were laid in **ruins** before the Lord, before His fierce anger. For thus says the Lord; The whole land shall be a desolation; yet I will not make a full end. Jer. 4:23-27

Mortal, eat your bread with **quaking**, and drink your water with **trembling** and with fearfulness.... The inhabited cities shall be laid waste, and the land shall become a desolation; and you shall know that I am the Lord. Ezek. 12:17,20

He **shatters** the doors of bronze, and cuts in two the bars of iron. Ps. 107:16

You shall **break** them with a rod of iron, and **dash** them **in pieces** like a potter's vessel. Ps. 2:9

To everyone who conquers and continues to do My works to the end, I will give authority over the nations; to rule them with an iron rod, as when clay pots are **shattered**.

Rev. 2:26-27

For thus says the Lord of hosts: Once again, in a little while, I will **shake** the heavens and the earth and the sea and the dry land; and I will **shake** all the nations, so that the treasure of all nations shall come. Haggai 2:6-7

I am about to **shake** the heavens and the earth, and to overthrow the throne of kingdoms; I am about to destroy the strength of the kingdoms of the nations, and **overthrow** the chariots and their riders; the horses and their riders shall **fall**.... Haggai 2:21-22

Therefore I will make the heavens **tremble**, and the earth will be **shaken** out of its place, at the wrath of the Lord of hosts in the day of His fierce anger. Is. 13:13

At that time His voice **shook** the earth; but now He has promised, "Yet once more I will **shake** not only the earth but also the heaven" ...[which] indicates the removal of what is **shaken**...so that what cannot be **shaken** may remain. Heb. 12:26-27

O that My people would listen to Me.... Then those who hate the Lord would **cringe** before Him, and their doom would last forever. Ps. 81:15

Then all the princes of the sea shall step down from their thrones; they shall remove their robes and strip off their embroidered garments. They shall clothe themselves with **trembling**, and shall sit on the ground; they shall **tremble** every moment. Ezek. 26:16

Wail, for the day of the Lord is near; it will come like destruction from the Almighty! Therefore all hands will be **feeble**, and every human heart will **melt**, and they will be **dismayed**. Pangs and agony will seize them; they will be in anguish like a woman in labor. They will look aghast at one another; their faces will be aflame. Is. 13:6-8

At Your rebuke, O God of Jacob, both rider and horse lay **stunned**. Ps. 76:4

His way is in **whirlwind** and storm, and the clouds are the dust of His feet.... The mountains **quake** before Him, and the hills melt; **the earth heaves** before Him, the world and all who live in it. Who can stand before His indignation? Who can endure the heat of His anger? His wrath is poured out like fire, and by Him the rocks **are broken** in pieces.

Nahum 1:3-6

His breath is like an overflowing stream that reaches up to the neck—to **sift** the nations with the sieve of destruction. Is. 30:28

He has stretched out His hand over the sea, He has **shaken** the kingdoms; the Lord has given command. Is. 23:11

Remember this is God's Word, not any man's idea, and it is what comes *after* these heaven shattering things that we are longing to see take place—the majestic, glorious return and reign of our Redeemer and Bridegroom, JESUS!

It is like praying for a baby to be born. In desiring the baby to come we are asking for the pain and travail of the birthing process. In fact, Jesus uses this as His illustration. *"And there will be famines and earthquakes in various places; all this is but the beginning of the birth pangs."* Matt. 24:8

David and Isaiah prayed for such things to take place. *Bow your heavens, O Lord, and come down; touch the mountains so that they smoke. Ps. 144:5-6*

*O that You would tear open the heavens and come down, so that the mountains would **quake** at Your presence, as when... [the melting fire burns (kjv, nkjv)], and the fire causes the waters to boil, to make Your Name known...! Is. 64:1-2*

We can pray like them. And we can also use Jesus' Words to pray that the labor pains be shortened. *"And unless those days were shortened, no flesh would be saved; but for the elect's sake those days will be shortened."* Matt. 24:22 NKJV

But woe to the earth and the sea, for the devil has come down to you with great wrath, because he knows that his time is short! (Rev. 12:12). So let's pray that the devils time be made really short! And pray that people will not be deceived and *that the nations might tremble at [His] presence* in reverence and repentance.

Next we see God is also going to shake and remove the hosts of heaven referring to the demons. Again, may we tremble with awe and worship.

On that day I will punish the host of heaven in heaven. Is. 24:21

When My sword has drunk its fill in heaven…. Is. 34:5

The Lord will be terrible against them; He will **shrivel** all the gods of the earth.

Zeph. 2:11

All the host of heaven shall rot away, and the skies roll up like a scroll. All their host shall **wither** like a leaf withering on a vine, or fruit withering on a fig tree. Is. 34:4

Therefore I will **shake** the heavens…. Is. 13:13 NKJV

And the stars of the sky **fell** to the earth as the fig tree drops its winter fruit when **shaken** by a gale. The sky vanished like a scroll rolling itself up, and every mountain and island was removed from its place. Rev. 6:13-14

And a **violent earthquake** such as had not occurred since there were people on the earth, so violent was that earthquake…. and every island fled away, and no mountains were to be found; huge hailstones…**dropped** from heaven…. Rev. 16:18,20

There will be signs in the sun, the moon, and the stars, and on the earth distress among the nations confused by the roaring of the sea and the waves. People will **faint** from fear and foreboding of what is coming upon the world, for the powers of the heavens will be **shaken**. Lk. 21:25-26

Immediately after the suffering of those days the sun will be darkened and the moon will not give its light; the stars will **fall** from heaven, and the powers of heaven will be **shaken**.

Matt. 24:29

Work out your own salvation with fear and **trembling.** Phil. 2:12

The king trusts in the Lord; through the unfailing Love of the Most High he will not be **shaken**. Ps. 21:7 NIV

Those who trust in the Lord…cannot be **shaken** but endure forever. Ps. 125:1 NIV

Prayers about Trembling

O Yeshua Adonai, You are so awesome. We tremble in Your presence. We quiver in reverent fear at Your Greatness. I tremble in awe that You, who are so Great and Mighty, long to have a relationship with me. Keep me always in this trembling attitude of reverent awe, Yeshua. Shake as much as You need to shake in my life to keep me here.

May all people on the earth come to know Your Power and Might. Shake all that is around them until they see the Truth that You are greater than they are; that You are Mightier than anything they know; that You are the Most High, and we are but dust. May they see Your Power and tremble at Your Name! May they be shaken until all that is not of You—all that does not respect You or honor You—will crumble and fall away. Let all the people of the world be shaken until all their strongholds are demolished and they are set free. Shake us until we all tremble before You in pure awe and reverence for You. So that You may be worshiped in the honor You deserve, for You are worthy of ALL Glory and ALL praise!

Sept. 29, '05

Jesus, please remove stubbornness and rebellion from us. Please make a way—find a way to get to us so we will all repent of our rebellion and stubbornness. Our whole nation, Jesus, the Liberals and the ACLU! The WHOLE WORLD!! The Muslims leaders! The TERRORISTS! O God, pierce all their hearts until they repent of their wicked rebellion, stubbornness, deceitfulness, blindness, and their anti-Christ spirits. Send Your Word that will pierce and prick their hearts. Send Your shaking that will shake and shatter their foundations. Send Your Fire that will burn into their dead consciences. Turn them to YOU, JESUS, their SAVIOR!!

June 2, '06

I was just thinking that the reason so many people accepted the Gospel at the time of Pentecost (8000 in the first few days alone!) could be because of all they had just gone through. Here's a list of all the events.

1. *When it was noon, darkness came over the whole land [note: or earth] until three in the afternoon* (Mk. 15:33). *...while the sun's light failed* (Lk. 23:44). So it was not from a storm or from clouds; the sun just stopped shining! Pretty scary! And in their synagogues they read through the Old Testament every year, so they would've heard these verses many times: *On that day, says the Lord God, I will make the sun go down at noon, and darken the earth in broad daylight* (Amos 8:9) and *The earth shall mourn and the heavens above grow black.* (Jer. 4:23). Quite jolting!

2. *At that moment...the earth shook and rocks were split* (Matt. 27:51). That's a big earthquake! How frightening!

3. *The tombs also were opened, and many bodies of the saints...were raised* (Matt. 27:51-52). (Open tombs with dead people moving around in them? Scary indeed!)

4. ***The*** curtain, which was a couple stories tall, and was extremely thick was torn, and not by human hands! This was in *the* temple—their world famous, magnificent temple. This would've been big news. Everyone would have been talking about it. And they would've known about other things in the Old Testament happening without human hands, like the writing on the wall.

5. Then three days later *...as the first day of the week was dawning, ...suddenly there was a **great earthquake*** (Matt. 28:1-2). This would have been on the morning of the Festival of the Firstfruits while they were bringing their baskets of first fruits to the temple that now had a torn curtain!

6. *After His resurrection they* [the dead saints] *came out of the tombs and entered the holy city and appeared to many* (Matt. 27:53). (Maybe they suddenly appeared like Jesus did. Even more scary!)

7. Then 50 days later when they were all in Jerusalem for another Holy Day: *Suddenly from heaven there came a sound like the rush of a violent wind...and at the sound the crowd gathered* (Acts 2:2,6). This horrible sound came down out of the sky! Quite alarming!

They would've been pretty shaken up and scared by then, you'd think, because besides the big news of the famous man they thought was the Messiah (who really was!) being crucified, and the rumors of Him rising again, there had been a weird darkness, a huge earthquake, the curtain torn, another big earthquake, people coming out of opened tombs and making sudden appearances, and now a weird, violent sound—and all these on festival days! Maybe that's why they were ready to repent and receive Yeshua as their Mashiach (Messiah).

So, Yeshua, let it happen again. Bring however many spectacular things You need to bring to this world to make people ready and open by the thousands and millions to receive You. Make things happen in succession, the whole world over, that will make every heart tender with trembling fear—ready to be rescued and saved by You—ready in the way that they know they need to be rescued and will gladly receive Your salvation as the answer!! Let it happen, Yeshua. This time may it even shake the hypocritical leaders and rulers!! Even the terrorist leaders!! ALL of them so *they* will receive You, too!

Persevere in prayer. Romans 12:12

Prophecies
about the Coastlands

The coastlands are where most of the big cities are in the world. In America it is where the philosophy of liberalism has the strongest hold. It is also where cities that are famous for their sin are, such as San Francisco, which is known for its homosexual community, and New Orleans for its Mardi Gras reveling. Also some coastlands are Muslim strongholds. So, to have the coastlands turn to God will take an astronomical miracle and a lot of warfare praying. These Scriptures can be wonderful weapons for such prayer battles.

He will not grow faint or be crushed until He has established justice in the earth; and the **coastlands** wait for His teaching. Is. 42:4

Listen to Me, O **coastlands,** pay attention, you peoples from far away! Is. 49:1

The **coastlands** shall wait for Me.... Is. 60:9
The **coastlands** wait for Me, and for My arm they hope. Is. 51:5b

The Lord is king! Let the earth rejoice; let the many **coastlands** be glad! Ps. 97:1

Listen to Me in silence, O **coastlands**; let the peoples renew their strength; let them approach, then let them speak; let us together draw near for judgment.... Is. 41:1

I, the Lord, am first, and will be with the last. The **coastlands** have seen and are afraid, the ends of the earth tremble; they have drawn near and come. Is. 41: 1,4-5

To the **coastlands**, He will render requital. Is. 59:18
To the **coastlands** far away that have not heard of My fame or seen My Glory and they shall declare My Glory. Is. 66:18
The Lord, ...to Him shall bow down, each in its place, all the **coasts** and **islands** of the nations. Zeph. 2:11

Sing to the Lord a new song, His praise from the end of the earth! Let the sea roar and all that fills it, the **coastlands** and their inhabitants. Let the desert and its towns lift up their voice...let them shout from the tops of the mountains. Let them give Glory to the Lord, and declare His praise in the **coastlands**. Is. 42:10-12

Prayer about Coastlands

O Yeshua Adonai, we war with You to defeat the enemy who has such a hold on all the coastlands:

In Yeshua's Holy Name we bind the enemy in chains and fetters, and we speak to him to be removed and cast into hell. By the Power of Yeshua's Blood, we silence all his lies and deceit, and speak to them to be shriveled up to nothing. By Yeshua's resurrection power, we pray for the revelation and Truth of Yeshua to be revealed in all coastlands to all people dwelling there. May they all be drawn to the Truth and embrace it.

May all these prophecies about the coastlands come to pass, Yeshua. May the coastlands wait for Your teaching. May they learn Your ways. May all the coastlands declare Your praise. Hallelujah! Glory!

Nov. 2, '05

(Written after watching the DVD, *The Cross—Jesus in China,* produced by The Voice of the Martyrs.) (You watch it. You will get excited, too!)

It's been true, Jesus! It's been what has happened! *They shout from the west over the majesty of the Lord, therefore in the east give glory to the Lord; in the* **coastlands of the sea** *glorify the Name of the Lord.* Is. 24:14-15

Hallelujah! Your Word has been coming to pass! It started in the West and it has spread through missionaries to the East—to China!

Lord, make it stronger in the coastlands!

Strong peoples will glorify You (Is. 25:3). O yes, Jesus, bring it to pass!! Oh I'm overwhelmed with joy! You shall bring it to pass!

For He has done gloriously! Let this be known in all the earth! (Is. 12:3,5). Hallelujah! Amen!

First of all...I urge that supplications, prayers, intercessions, and thanksgivings be made for everyone, for kings and all who are in high positions. I Tim.2:1

Prophecies
about
Nations, Peoples,
and the
Ends of the Earth

These promises in this section fill my heart with pure joy! I'm tickled that they are actually in the Bible. What awesome prophetic weapons. Please join me in launching them in this exciting attack against the enemy. Let's battle with our wonderful, loving Commander who wants all nations to come to know Him and become His people.

"For God **so** loved the **world**." Jn. 3:16 (He loves the world so, very much!)

"He gave his only Son...that the **world** might be saved through Him." Jn. 3:16,17

"...You have given Him authority over all people to give eternal life to all..." Jn. 17:2

[Jesus praying to the Father] "So that the **world** may believe that You have sent Me.... So that the **world** may know that You have sent Me and have loved them." Jn. 17:21,23

Let this be recorded for a generation to come, so that a **people** yet unborn [NKJV: yet to be created] may praise the Lord. Ps. 102:18

"Thus it is written, ...that repentance and forgiveness of sins is to be proclaimed in [Jesus] Name to **all nations**...." Lk. 24:46,47

"Go therefore and make disciples of **all nations**...teaching them to obey everything I have commanded." Matt. 28:19

"Go into all the **world** and proclaim the Good News to the **whole creation**." Mk. 16:15

"And you will be My witnesses...to the **ends of the earth**." Acts 1:8

"And this Good News of the kingdom will be proclaimed **throughout the world,** as a testimony to **all the nations**; and then the end will come." Matt. 24:14

I will give you as a light to the **nations**, that My salvation may reach to the **end of the earth**. Is. 49:6

Make known His deed among the **nations**. Sing praises to the Lord for He has done gloriously, let this be known in **all the earth**. Is. 12:3,5

Ask of Me, and I will make the **nations** your heritage, and the **ends of the earth** your possession. Ps. 2:8 {God is commanding us here! So we had better begin asking!}

May **all kings** bow down before [You]; all **nations** give [You] service. Ps. 72:11

Kings of the earth and **all peoples**, princes and **all rulers of the earth**! Young men and women alike, old and young together! Let them praise the Name of the Lord, for His Name alone is exalted; His Glory is above earth and heaven. Ps. 148:11-13

That Your ways may be known on earth; Your salvation among **all nations**,
May the **peoples** praise You, may the **nations** be glad and sing for joy.
May the **peoples** praise You, O God, may **all the peoples** praise You.
Then the earth shall yield its harvest, and God, our God, will bless us,
God will bless us and all the **ends of the earth** will fear Him [NRSV: revere Him].
Ps. 67:2-7 NIV

The **nations** shall fear the Name of the Lord, and **all the kings of the earth** Your Glory. Ps. 102:15

All the nations You have made shall come and bow down [NIV and KJV: worship] before You, O Lord, and shall Glorify Your Name. Ps. 86:9

Sing to the Lord a new song, His praise from **the end of the earth**!... The desert and its towns lift up their voice. Is. 42:10,11 {I love this verse because it includes the desert country of Mongolia where I ministered once!}

I heard...the voice of **a great multitude** like the sound of many waters, like the sound of mighty thunder peals crying out, "Hallelujah, for the Lord our God the Almighty reigns.
Rev. 19:6

Ah, the thunder of many **peoples**, they thunder like the thundering of the sea! Ah the roar of **nations**, they roar like the roaring of mighty waters! The **nations** roar like the roaring of many waters. Is. 17:12-13

The floods have lifted up, O Lord
The floods have lifted up their voice.
The floods lift up their roaring,
More majestic than the thunders of mighty waters
More majestic than the waves of the sea,
Majestic on high is the Lord. Ps. 93:3-4
{Perhaps these "floods" are the multitudes in Revelation and Isaiah above.}

I will thank You in the great congregation; in the **mighty throng** I will praise You.
Ps. 35:17-18

Praise the Lord, **all you nations**! Extol Him, **all you peoples**. Ps. 117:1
Peoples gather together, and **kingdoms**, to worship the Lord. Ps. 102:22

The Lord is great in Zion; He is exalted over **all the peoples**, let them praise Your great and awesome Name! Holy is He! Ps. 99:2-3

All the **kings of the earth** shall praise You, O Lord, for they have heard the Words of Your mouth. They shall sing of the ways of the Lord, for great is the Glory of the Lord.
Ps. 138:4

They lift up their voices. They sing for joy; they shout from the west over the Majesty of the Lord. Therefore in the east give Glory to the Lord; in the coastlands of the sea Glorify the Name of the Lord, the God of Israel. From the **ends of the earth** we hear songs of praise, of Glory to the Righteous One. Is. 24:14-16

The heavens declare the Glory of God. The skies proclaim the work of His hands. Day after day they pour forth speech, night after night they display knowledge. There is no speech, nor are there words; their voice is not heard; yet their voice goes out through all the earth, and their words to the **end of the world**. Ps. 19:1-4

Ever since the creation of the **world** His eternal Power and Divine nature, invisible though they are, have been understood and seen through the things He has made. So they are without excuse. Rom. 1:20

Draw near, O **nations**, to hear; O **peoples** give heed! Let the earth hear and all that fills it; the **world** and all that comes from it. Is. 34:1

Listen to Me, O coastlands, pay attention, you **peoples** from far away! Is. 49:1

Turn to Me and be saved, all the **ends of the earth**! For I am God, and there is no other. Is. 45:22

The Lord has bared His holy arm before the eyes of all the **nations**; and all the **ends of the earth** shall see the salvation of our God. Is. 52:10

On that day p**eople** will regard their Maker and their eyes will look to the Holy One. Is. 17:7

Therefore **strong peoples** will glorify You; cities of ruthless **nations** will fear You. Is. 25:3

Nations shall come to Your light and **kings** to the brightness of Your dawn. Is. 60:3

So that they may know, from the rising of the sun and from the west, that there is no one besides Me; I am the Lord, and there is no other. Is. 45:6

My Name will be great among the **nations**, from the rising to the setting of the sun. In **every place** incense and pure offerings will be brought to My Name, because My Name will be great among the **nations**," says the Lord Almighty. Mal. 1:11 NIV

So those in the west shall fear the Name of the Lord, and those in the east, His Glory. Is. 59:19

For as the earth brings forth its shoots, and as a garden causes what is sown in it to spring up, so the Lord God will cause righteousness and praise to spring up before **all the nations**. Is. 61:11

Be still and know that I am God. I will be exalted among the **nations** [KJV: heathen] I will be exalted in the **earth**. Ps. 46:10 NIV

I will sanctify My great Name, ... and the **nations** shall know that I am the Lord, says the Lord God, when through you I display My holiness before their eyes. Ezek. 36:23

I will display My Glory among the **nations**; and **all the nations** shall see My judgment that I have executed, and My hand that I have laid on them. Ezek. 39:21

For I know their works and their thoughts and I am coming to gather **all nations** and tongues; and they shall come and shall see My Glory.... To the coastlands far away that have not heard of My fame or seen My Glory and they shall declare My Glory among the **nations**,.... From new moon to new moon and from Sabbath to Sabbath **ALL flesh** shall come to worship before Me, says the Lord. Is. 66:18,19,23

O Lord, my strength and my stronghold...to You shall the **nations** come from the **ends of the earth** and say: Our ancestors have inherited nothing but lies, worthless things in which there is no profit. ... "Therefore I am going to teach them,,,My Power and My Might, and they shall know that My Name is the Lord." Jer. 16:19-21

And there was **a great multitude** that **no one could count**, from **every nation**, from **all tribes** and **peoples** and **languages**, standing before the throne and before the Lamb, robed in white...saying, "Salvation belongs to our God...and to the Lamb!" Rev. 7:9-10

To Him was given dominion and glory and kingship, that **all peoples**, **nations**, and **languages** should serve Him. Dan. 7:14

Then I heard **every creature** in heaven and on earth and under the earth and in the sea, and all that is in them, singing, "To the One seated on the throne and to the Lamb be blessing and honor and glory and might forever and ever." Rev. 5:13

The Lord, ...to Him shall bow down, each in its place, all the coasts and islands of the **nations**. Zeph. 2:11

At the Name of Jesus **every** knee [shall] bow in heaven and on earth and under the earth, and **every** tongue [shall] confess that Jesus Christ is Lord, to the glory of God the Father. Phil. 2:10-11 (The Greek word can mean "shall" so I put "shall.")

Assemble yourselves and come together, draw near, you survivors of the **nations**! ...By Myself I have sworn, from My mouth has gone forth in righteousness a Word that shall not return: "To Me **every** knee shall bow, **every** tongue shall swear." Is. 45:20, 23

"...Every knee shall bow...and every tongue shall give praise to God." Rom. 14:11

My Name is reverenced among the **nations**. Mal. 1:14b

All the **ends of the earth** shall remember and turn to the Lord; and all the families of the **nations** shall worship before Him.... Future generations will be told about the Lord, and proclaim deliverance to a people yet unborn. Ps. 22:27,30-31

All the earth worships You [NIV: bows down to You]; they sing praises to You...come and see what God has done. Ps. 66:4-5

At that time I will change the speech of the **peoples** to a pure speech, that **all of them** may call on the Name of the Lord and serve Him with one accord. Zeph. 3:9

God my King is from of old, working salvation in the **earth**. Ps. 74:12

Let all the **earth** fear the Lord; let all the inhabitants of the **world** stand in awe of Him. Ps. 33:8

Prayer for the Nations

O Yeshua Adonai, be exalted among the nations! Let Your Word come to pass that You will be exalted in all the earth!! Thank you, Father, that You Love the nations, that Your Love is so great that You gave Your Son as a ransom for the whole world. I pray this Good News will be proclaimed throughout the world, as Your Word promises! Thank You that it is being done! Your people are working now to accomplish it. Empower them to persevere, Holy Spirit. Inspire them. Anoint them. Make all their work prosperous. Make all their efforts fruitful. Give them abundant harvests wherever You send them—even to the ends of the earth!

Yeshua, we ask You as You commanded us to do. Please give us the nations as our inheritance. We want no other inheritance, Yeshua, only this, that all the nations may come to know You and worship You. Give all the nations—every last one—to us, Your people.

O Yeshua, we wage warfare with these Scriptures. May all the kings and all the rulers from every country, province, and state (Your promises say "all," Yeshua!) bow down and worship You. May men and women, young and old, the whole world over, come to know You and accept You as Lord, and praise You.

Lord, even strong and ruthless nations shall see Your Might and Power, and shall melt with fear, and turn to You in repentance. And their speech shall be pure in their praise to YOU. Praise Your Name, Jesus/Yeshua. Bring it to pass by the Power of Your Love! All flesh shall worship You, Father! Thank You that it shall be so.

I thank You that those who worship You shall be a multitude so huge that no one can count the number. Thank You, Yeshua. May it be all the people who ever lived. May satan rob no one from Your kingdom! May Your Kingdom come and Your will be done on earth as it is in Heaven! Amen! So be it!

Nov. 18, '02

Jesus, the movie media is the most powerful media in all the earth. No one ever gets tired of watching movies. They are never done viewing! Teenagers, men, women, none of them ever say, "I'm sick of movies. I don't ever want to watch another movie ever again."

People are getting saturated by the messages of the movies, Jesus. It is what is putting a shroud over their minds so they don't come to know you (Is. 25:7). It is what is teaching people to think and walk in darkness. The devil is using it to expand his kingdom.

But I want to claim the movie media for Your Kingdom, Jesus. Use it, Jesus! Use it for Your Kingdom and Your Glory!! Use it to reach the whole world for You. I take it back from the enemy in Your Name, Jesus. I command it to be loosed from the devil's hold and I claim it for Your kingdom only—only for You, Jesus!! We claim it all for You. Let it be like the angel of Revelation 14:6 who carries the Gospel to every tribe and tongue.

O Jesus, please bring forth a series of movies, books and TV shows—a whole long series that captivates the world even more than the Left Behind series did. Jesus, inspire people—100's of people—Your people—to create the one series or several series that will be an absolute sensation, that will draw the masses to the movies, to the bookstores, to the TV, that will cause them to give up all their other shows and movies and entertainment. O Jesus, create the story line. Cause it to be written and produced. O Jesus, a series so powerful that it will be full of Your powerful WORD that it will be sharper than any two-edged sword—that it WILL reveal ALL the thoughts and intents of every heart—that it will water the earth—that it will accomplish Your purpose—that it will bring all the billions to You, Jesus—all the billions of the people on this earth. I pray that all will be able to see the movies and read the books and Your LIGHT will shine in their hearts and they will repent and receive You and dedicate their whole lives to You, and the series will teach them how to walk with You and will turn them to Your WORD for their life sustenance. O Jesus, please let it be so.

Inspire Your people, Jesus. Some are inspired. Inspire 100's and 1000's more, Jesus. May the airways and theaters be flooded with Your movies—with Your WORD—with top-notch creativity unable to be touched by the ungodly talent. May Your movies be so awesome that no one will desire ungodly ones anymore!!! Their hearts will be turned to You and to Your Way. They will be repulsed by evil and immorality and ungodliness. They will only be hungry and thirsty for righteousness!!

Thank you, Jesus, for how *The JESUS Film* is reaching the world. Keep blessing it, Jesus. Keep blessing it. But it doesn't appeal to Americans. Please inspire movies using Your Word that impress Americans and Europeans, too, Jesus.

And Jesus, please I pray that You will win, not satan. I pray ALL people will come to know You and worship You as Your Word promises!!! I pray satan will get NO ONE!!!

June 19, '04

Jesus, keep using movies and the media to bring people to You. Please use movies to cause people to purify themselves and worship You. Use all media, Jesus. Purify all media. Take back all media for Your purposes and Your Glory. Use the news. Thank you for using the news at Reagan's funeral to proclaim the Gospel to the whole WORLD(!!) and to lift up Godly marriage to the world.

Dec. 6, '04

On Oct. 6, '04 God gave me the verse, *O Lord God...let it be known this day that you are God in Israel, that I am your servant, and that I have done all these things at your bidding* (I Kings 18:36). I sense that this is what I am to ask today.

Lord, let it be known that You are God in America. Jesus, let it be known that You are King of Kings and Lord of Lords in this world, in the USA, in church, in Iraq, in China, in the WORLD. Let it be known that Your WORD is powerful, living, and active—that Your Word stands and that Your Word is TRUTH, encompassing all truth and overthrowing all falsehood. Let it be known that You have a plan and that YOU WILL DO IT and that we are Your servants, and that little, measly I am actually YOUR servant, and that we have done all these things at Your BIDDING—all the things You are calling us to do.

Aug. 19, '02

O Lord Jesus, Savior of the world, I pray Your Will will be done in the nations of this earth as it is in Heaven. As the missionary Chris Antoinette said, we break the curses we've spoken over them, saying they are Hindi, or Buddhist, or heathen, or third world. We renounce all those terms which we have assigned to them for generations. We break all curses over them—all faithless words over them—and we speak the blessings of God's kingdom coming to them.

By the redeeming power of Your Blood, Jesus, make India a Christian nation. Wipe out Hinduism and Buddhism. Make Africa a pure Christian continent. Wipe out heathenism, satanism, tribalism, and babarianism. And please wipe out the AIDS disease there.

Make China a strong Christian nation—a pure, sweet, Godly Nation. Wipe out Buddhism, Taoism, ancestor worship, and communism. Wipe out materialism and worship of science. Wipe out Darwinism and atheism. Flood China with Your LOVE and POWER and HOLINESS!

Wipe out Islam and Jihad in the Middle East. Break the stronghold it has on its people.

I pray for Japan, Jesus. Wipe out Buddhism and the worship of the emperor and ancestors. Break the hardness of their hearts against Christianity. Soften their hearts for Your Word. Let them know that to turn to You makes them more Japanese not less. May Japan become fertile soil for Your seed, Jesus. Bring forth an abundant harvest there.

I pray for all nations. Indonesia and the Philippines. Australia—strengthen and purify it. America—bring it to complete repentance and holiness before You, Jesus. England, Germany, Spain, France, Italy, Russia, Ukraine, Ireland, on and on. All Nations, Jesus. May they all become nations that worship You.

Mar. 6, '06

Lord, I pray for a fire to be kindled among the Muslims—the fire of Your Holy Spirit. Let it catch on and spread rapidly throughout the whole religion of Islam across country borders from the richest to the poorest, from the moderates to the fanatic Jihadists. And let the fire be fanned and kept burning with discipleship materials and discipling. Let it be followed with a sincere, devoted-to-Your-Word-and-Your-Kingdom zeal and on-fire spirit. A spirit of wisdom and revelation, and a spirit of holiness.

Mar. 23, '06

*"...You have given Him authority over **all people** to give eternal life to **all**."* Jn.17:2

God gave Jesus authority over **all people** to give eternal life to **all!!!**

O Yeshua/Jesus, You have authority to give eternal life to all people. O may You be able to do that. May all people receive Your eternal LIFE!! May every last person receive it!

[After several years of hearing my earnest prayers for the nations, God started doing a spectacular thing for me. He started sending *me* to the nations to help spread the Gospel, to be able to pray on site, and to witness what God was already doing there. I was amazed to see how much He *is* doing, especially in Africa. I got to go to China, Thailand, Kenya, Tanzania, El Salvador, Israel, and even Mongolia which truly is the end of the earth. So let's be encouraged to keep on pouring our hearts out in prayer for the nations. Besides answering our prayers, who knows what else God will do.]

O God.... Remember how the impious scoff at You all day long. Psalms 74:22

Words about the World's Wisdom and Leadership

Let's pray these Scriptures against all the deceitful leaders of today who are fighting against God and the Truth. Remember it is their foolish, so-called "wisdom" that we are praying to be brought down, so that the people themselves will repent and be saved. Let's also use these verses to examine ourselves and get rid of our own foolish thinking.

Whoever...does not agree with the sound Words of our Lord Jesus...is conceited, understanding nothing, and has a morbid craving for controversy.... I Tim. 6:3-4

For the message about the cross is foolishness to those who are perishing, but to us...it is the POWER OF GOD. I Cor. 1:18

The Word of the Lord is to them an object of scorn; they take no pleasure in it. Jer. 6:10

Those who are unspiritual do not receive the gifts of God's Spirit, for they are foolishness to them, and they are unable to understand them because they are spiritually discerned. I Cor. 2:14

They slander what they do not understand. II Pet. 2:12

They have no sense; for they do not know the way of the Lord, the Law of their God. ...They all alike had broken the yoke, they had burst the bonds. Jer. 5:4-5

For My people are foolish. They do not know Me; they are stupid children, they have no understanding. They are skilled in doing evil, but do not know how to do good. Is. 4:22

For though they knew God, they did not honor Him as God or give thanks to Him, but they became futile in their thinking, and their senseless minds were darkened. Rom. 1:21

Professing themselves to be wise, they became fools. Rom. 1:22 KJV

Fools say in their hearts, "There is no God." Ps. 14:1

Take heed, you senseless ones among the people; you fools, when will you become wise?.... Does He who teaches man lack knowledge? The Lord knows the thoughts of man. Ps. 94:8,10-11 NIV

Your wisdom and your knowledge led you astray. Is. 47:10

The Lord knows the thoughts of man, that they are but an empty breath. Ps. 94:11

"The Lord knows the thoughts of the wise, that they are futile." I Cor. 3:20

The mind of the wicked is of little worth. Prov. 10:20

Everyone is stupid and without knowledge.... They are worthless, a work of delusion; at the time of their punishment they shall perish. Jer. 51:17,18

Because they...did not choose the fear of the Lord, would have none of My counsel, and despised all My reproof, therefore they shall...be sated with their own devices. For...the complacency of fools destroys them. Prov. 1:29-32

And since they did not see fit to acknowledge God, God gave them up to a debased mind. Rom. 1:28

The best of them is like a brier, the most upright...a thorn hedge. Mic. 7:4

They refused to love the Truth and so be saved. For this reason God sends them a powerful delusion, leading them to believe what is false, so that all who have not believed the Truth but took pleasure in unrighteousness will be condemned. II Thess. 2:11-12

For you are from your father, the devil, and you choose to do your father's desires. Jn. 8:44

From prophet to priest everyone deals falsely. Jer. 6:13

How can you say, "We are wise, and the Law of the Lord is with us," when, in fact, the false pen of the scribes has made it a lie? Jer. 8:8

They bend their tongues like bows; they have grown strong in the land for falsehood and not for truth; ...and they do not know Me, says the Lord. Jer. 9:3

No one speaks the truth; they have taught their tongues to speak lies.... They refuse to know Me, says the Lord.... Their tongue is a deadly arrow; it speaks deceit through the mouth.... Shall I not punish them for these things? says the Lord; shall I not bring retribution on a nation such as this? Jer. 9:5,6,8,9

For there is no truth in their mouths.... Make them bear their guilt, O God; let them fall by their own counsels; because of their many transgressions cast them out, for they have rebelled against You. Ps. 5:9-10

Let the lying lips be stilled.... Ps. 31:18

Let the...lips be stilled...that speak insolently against righteousness.... Ps. 31:18

Let the...lips be stilled...that speak...with pride and contempt. Ps. 31:18

Thus says the Lord concerning the prophets who lead My people astray...the seers shall be disgraced, and the diviners put to shame; they shall all cover their lips. Micah 3:5,7

The wise shall be put to shame, they shall be dismayed and taken; since they have rejected the Word of the Lord, what wisdom is in them? Therefore I will give their wives to others. Jer. 8:9

I am the Lord, who...frustrates the omens of liars, and makes fools of diviners; who turns back the wise and makes their knowledge foolish; who confirms the Word of His servant, and fulfills the prediction of His messengers. Is. 44:24-25

It is written, "I will destroy the wisdom of the wise; and the discernment of the discerning I will thwart." ...Has not God made foolish the wisdom of the world? I Cor. 1:19,20

For it is written, I will baffle and render useless and destroy the learning of the learned, and the philosophy of the philosophers, and the cleverness of the clever, and the discernment of the discerning, I will frustrate and nullify them and bring them to NOTHING.
I Cor. 1:19 Amp.

So I will again do amazing things with this people, shocking and amazing. The wisdom of their wise shall perish, and the discernment of the discerning shall be hidden.
Is. 29:14

I will confound their plans. Is. 19: 3

I am the Lord...who turns back the wise, and makes their knowledge foolish.
Is. 44:24, 25

Where is the philosopher, ...scholar, ...investigator, logician, debater...of this age? Has not God shown up the nonsense and folly of this world's wisdom? I Cor. 1:20 AMP.

The Lord foils the plans of the nations; He thwarts the purposes of the peoples.
Ps. 33:10 NIV

Those who devise evil He condemns. Prov. 12:2

He catches the wise in their craftiness. I Cor. 3:19

He [God] frustrates the devices of the crafty, so that their hands achieve no success. He takes the wise in their own craftiness; and the schemes of the wily are brought to a quick end. Job 5:12

Let them be turned back and confounded who devise evil, Ps. 35:4

Let the wicked fall into their own nets... Ps. 141:10

Let the net that they hid ensnare them; let them fall in it—to their ruin. Ps. 35:8

Those who mislead the upright into evil ways will fall into pits of their own making. Prov. 28:10

Whoever digs a pit will fall into it, and a stone will come back on the one who starts it rolling. Prov. 26:27

They make a pit, digging it out, and fall into the hole that they have made. Ps. 7:15

The nations have sunk in the pit that they made; in the net that they hid has their own foot been caught. Ps. 9:15

The Lord has poured into them a spirit of confusion. Is. 19:14

All of them are put to shame and confounded, [they] go in confusion together. Is. 45:16

The way of human beings is not in their control, ...mortals as they walk cannot direct their steps. Jer. 10:23

If they plan evil against You (God), if they devise mischief, they will not succeed. For You will put them to flight...with Your bows. Ps. 21:11-12

The Lord brings the counsel of the nations to nothing; He frustrates the plans of the peoples. Ps. 33:10

They walked in their own counsel and looked backward rather than forward. Jer. 7:24

The wicked flee when no one pursues. Prov. 28:1

Do not call conspiracy all that this people calls conspiracy, and do not fear what it fears. Is. 8:12

What the wicked dread will come upon them. Prov. 10:24

These have chosen their own ways, and in their abominations they take delight; I also will choose to mock them, and bring upon them what they fear; because, when I called, no one answered, when I spoke, they did not listen; but they did what was evil in My sight, and chose what did not please Me. Is 66:3-4

None of the wicked shall understand. Dan. 12:10

None of the rulers of this age understood it. I Cor. 2:8 NIV

They do not know the thoughts of the Lord; they do not understand His plan. Mic. 4:11

They are a nation void of sense; there is no understanding in them. If they were wise, they would understand this; they would discern what the end would be. Deut. 32:28-29

Indeed to this very day...a veil lies over their minds, but when one turns to the Lord, the veil is removed. II Cor. 3:15

And He will destroy...the shroud that is cast over all peoples, the sheet that is spread over all nations. Is. 25:7

For since...the world did not know God through [their] wisdom, God decided, through the foolishness of our proclamation, to save those who believe. I Cor. 1:21

For when the world with all its earthly wisdom failed to perceive and recognize and know God by means of its own philosophy, God in His Wisdom was pleased through the foolishness of preaching...to save.... I Cor. 1:21 AMP

For God's foolishness is wiser than human wisdom. I Cor. 1:25

But it is indeed not a wisdom of this present age or of this world or of the leaders and rulers of this age, *who are being brought to nothing and are doomed to pass away* [NRSV: to perish]. I Cor. 2:6 AMP

"Every plant that My Heavenly Father has not planted will be uprooted." Matt. 15:13

"For nothing is hidden that will not be disclosed, nor is anything secret that will not become known and come to Light." Lk. 8:17

...and God's weakness is stronger than human strength. I Cor. 1:25

I will find out not the talk of these arrogant people, but the power. For the Kingdom of God depends not on talk but on POWER. I Cor. 4:19

For the message about the cross is ... the POWER OF GOD. I Cor. 1:18

Prayer about the World's Wisdom

O Adonai, it is true! The wisdom of this world is complete foolishness. The top, most educated, most intelligent people in the world cannot solve the Middle East problem. In spite of all their human wisdom, human efforts, and generous provision of millions upon millions of dollars, the situation just keeps getting worse and worse.

O Adonai Elohim, confound their human wisdom. Thwart their destructive, confusing plans. Bring them all to naught. Cause the world leaders to suddenly see how useless and foolish all their initiatives and talks have been. Open their eyes to the futility of it all and cause them to cry out for Your True Wisdom which comes from fearing and reverencing You, from sitting at Your feet and soaking in Your Word until our own ideas and opinions dissolve away and we are saturated with the Wisdom from above.

Nov. 3, '05

O Lord Jesus, my heart aches for the world this morning. The people in the world don't see clearly, Jesus. If they saw clearly, surely they would choose to follow You! On this earth we see through a glass darkly. We have that sheet and shroud over us blocking our view of You (Is. 25:7)

Please remove that shroud, Jesus—that veil (Paul talks about it in II Cor. 3:14-15. *But their minds are hardened. Indeed, to this very day… whenever* [Jesus Words] *are read a veil lies over their minds…. But when one turns to the Lord the veil is removed.*) Jesus, a veil is lying over the world's minds today—even over church-going people. Paul says only in Christ is it set aside. But even then, Jesus, we still all see through a glass darkly (I Cor 13:12 KJV). Help us, Jesus. How can people turn to You when they are blinded by a veil? How can they turn to You when judgments are delayed so long? O Jesus, I don't know how to express my heart.

If Your presence was here on earth in a much more powerful way. If Your angels came to leaders in brightness and glory, in front of all the people, and the angels declared the truth and exposed the lies. Jesus, if You removed leaders who were leading people astray. And if the cloud was removed from everyone's mind. And Your Word was proclaimed in Truth and purity and Your presence was here with Your powerful, heart-melting power. Surely then all people would follow You. Surely then we would give up, and do away with all hindrances, and truly follow You. Surely then Christians would agree together how to live.

[*And you will again see the distinction between the righteous and the wicked, between those who serve God and those who do not.* Mal. 3:18

Yes, Lord! Thank you, Jesus! That is what I pray. Let there be a distinction between those who follow You and those who do not. Let the whole world know which people You are pleased with and which You are not. Let all the lies be exposed and Your Truth declared!] (This part in [ ] was added to the original journal entry in Mar. 2006.)

O Jesus, may all people turn to You. May all people follow You.

O Jesus, please turn all: kings, presidents, prime ministers, chairmen, in all nations and tribes to You. Turn the elderly, middle aged, young adults, teenagers, children—turn them all to You, Jesus, PLEASE.

May all choose to feed themselves with You and Your Word and receive Life, instead of feeding on entertainment and "idle songs" (Amos 6:5) that bring slow death. Please, Jesus, please!

People are weighed down with the cares of this life. Help them, Jesus. Help people turn to You fully and completely—wholeheartedly! Help us all to constantly be focused on You. *And all of us with unveiled faces seeing the Glory of the Lord…are being transformed into His image from Glory to Glory* (II Cor. 3:18 NIV). Help everyone in the world, especially every Christian to stay totally, entirely focused on nothing but You, Jesus, gazing upon You so that we will all be transformed from "Glory to Glory" into Your IMAGE!

June 19, '04

Jesus, please awaken leaders in this country to the truth that it is evil to kill fetuses or harvest fetuses for the purpose of curing diseases. Open their eyes to the lie and falsity and the evil of it. Wipe out their plans and intentions. Ruin their message, Jesus. Quiet their mouths until they are ready to speak Your Truth and not the devil's lies. Please, Jesus, by the power of Your Blood!

Oct. 13, '03 (After visiting orphanages in China and Thailand)

Yesterday we visited the orphanage. I could not keep the tears from flowing. I could hardly keep from wailing. There were so many tiny babies—sixteen of them—teensy tiny babies whose mothers don't want them.

O Jesus, the whole world now throws babies away, either by abortion, or by actually throwing away a live-born baby! They do in the U.S., in Europe, in India, but maybe not in Africa.

[The orphanage in China had so many perfectly formed, beautiful newborn babies! Darling babies, mostly girls, whose mothers and fathers weren't there to adore them! In Thailand the fathers and relatives don't want them because the babies have a stigma disease—AIDS.

My heart cries out, Jesus. A scream wells up within me. God help the world! Save the world, Jesus! The whole world is as bad as Canaan was in sacrificing their children.

In Jesus' Name, I rebuke the enemy who is deceiving the world into thinking it is okay to discard their offspring. By the authority of Jesus Christ crucified, I speak to this horrific lie to be silenced, and to be removed from the nations and the minds of all people of the world. I speak the Truth of Jesus—the Word of Life to replace the lie. I speak Life—Resurrection Life to the babies of the world. I pray for the Spirit of Elijah—the Holy Spirit to come and turn the hearts of parents to their children—to their newborns and to their pre-born. O Jesus, flood people with Your Love and compassion for their own young.

O Holy Spirit bring conviction and repentance for this awful sin.] (Between the [ ] are words I was telling people and praying, but didn't have time, then, to write down.)

Sept. 17, '05

O Lord, darkness seems to be closing in on the world. It needs to be rescued. O Jesus, bring Your LIGHT to this world. Bring Your GLORY. Remove death and destruction and darkness. Make it all flee before You.

Shower, O Heavens, from above, and let the skies rain down righteousness; let the earth open, that salvation may spring up, and let it cause righteousness to sprout up also; I the Lord have created it. Is. 45:8

Oct. 23, '03 (After a trip to China)

O Jesus I am haunted about the bad light America has over the whole world through Hollywood. The verse *If then the light in you is darkness, how great is that darkness!* (Matt. 6:23) speaks of the world today. America is a light to the world, but it is shining out darkness, and O how great is that darkness!! The street vendors in China were full of the bloodiest and filthiest of American movies, Jesus! Even the remote villages had VCR's with which to watch American filth. It's all they know about our country. They think we live like what they see on the screen. They think our men want a mistress right away.

Jesus, even Christians propagate Hollywood! How great is our darkness! O Heavenly Father, forgive us for our dark sins. Forgive us for bringing darkness and evil to the world this way. O Father, bring America to repentance. O Jesus, the fact that the immoral movies and porn are such big business in America says it all. We are a wicked people! Cause us to truly repent and turn from our wicked ways. Cause us to clean up Hollywood and the whole movie and TV business. Cause repentance in all those in this business from the least to the greatest. Cause repentance in all the viewers, so the demand for the ungodly images comes to an end. O Holy Spirit, cause it to happen by Your convicting power. Set people free from their addiction to it. Bring them out of their dingy dungeons. Help them to see the dinginess. Open their eyes to see the filth for what it is, and to repent of having anything to do with it. Cause them to cry out to You for forgiveness, and to beg for deliverance!

O Thank you, Jesus, that You will bring this revival to America! Thank you, that You will cleanse our light, until it is Your Light—until we shine Your Light brightly like a country set on a hill.

April 5, '06

It is God who commanded Light to shine out of darkness who has shone in our hearts to give the Light of the knowledge of the Glory of God in the face of Jesus Christ. II Cor. 4:6 KJV

God commanded it. "Let there be Light!!!" It is God who still commands it!

O Dear God, our Heavenly Father, please command that Light to shine in the world today, into every heart. Please command it, Lord. Only You have authority over Your Light. Please, I beg for more of Your Light in the face of Jesus Christ/ Yeshua HaMashiach in the world, in my heart. Command it to shine more into my heart, Father, into every heart!!

If our Gospel is veiled, it is veiled to those who are perishing. II Cor. 4:3

The god of this world has blinded the minds of the unbelievers, to keep them from seeing the Light of the Gospel of the Glory of Christ. II Cor. 4:4

O Father, help us to overcome satan and all his power. You, through Jesus/Yeshua, gave us authority over all his power (Lk. 10:19). Help us to take command and to overcome him so he will stop blinding the people of this world. Help us to unite in unity and agreement, Yeshua, to band together and take our position of authority and banish him from the earth—banish him and all his hosts.

The prayer of the righteous is...effective. James 5:16

The Wisdom
of the Righteous

Pray that our world leaders and we ourselves will become wise with the wisdom of God. His wisdom comes from sitting at Jesus' feet and soaking in His Word, being enlightened by the power, guidance, and teaching of the Holy Spirit.

The Lord is exalted, He dwells on high; ...He will be the stability of your times, abundance of salvation, wisdom, and knowledge; the fear of the Lord is [NIV: the key to this]...treasure. Is. 33:5-6

For the Lord gives wisdom; from His mouth [His Word] comes knowledge and understanding. Prov. 2:6

It is the wisdom of God once hidden...now revealed to us by God...for our glorification, that is, to lift us into the Glory of His Presence. I Cor. 1: 20

If you abide in Me and My Words abide in you.... Jn. 15:7

My Child, if you accept My Words and treasure up My commandments [also the Word of God] within you, ...you will understand righteousness...for wisdom will come into your heart...and understanding will guard you. Prov. 2:1,9,12

It is I who answer and look after you.... Your faithfulness comes from Me. Those who are wise understand these things; those who are discerning know them. For the ways of the Lord are right, and the upright walk in them Hosea 14:8-9

They will sanctify My Name... and will stand in awe of the God of Israel and those who err in spirit will come to understanding, and those who grumble will accept instruction.
Is. 29:23-24

Just as the Lord...charged me, I now teach you statutes and ordinances.... You must observe them diligently, for this will show your wisdom and discernment. Deut. 4:5-6

They are well instructed; their God teaches them. Is. 28:26

Whoever walks with the wise becomes wise. Prov. 13:20

And all of us, with unveiled faces, [AMP: beholding in the Word of God] seeing the Glory of the Lord, as though reflected in a mirror, are being transformed into [His] IMAGE! [from GLORY TO GLORY!!! NIV] from one degree of Glory to another; for this comes from the Lord, the Spirit. II Cor. 3:18

He who sows to the Spirit, will of the Spirit reap everlasting life. Gal. 6:8 NKJV

Think over these things—understand and grasp their application—for the Lord will grant you FULL INSIGHT and understanding in EVERYTHING. II Tim. 2:7 AMP.

The Spirit of Truth...will guide you into all Truth [which is wisdom!]. Jn. 16:13

The Holy Spirit will teach you everything. Jn. 14:26

God is faithful, by Him you were called into the fellowship of His Son, JESUS CHRIST OUR LORD. I Cor. 1:9

You are not lacking in any spiritual gift as you wait for the revealing of our Lord JESUS CHRIST. I Cor. 1:7

The unfolding of Your **Words** gives light; it imparts understanding to the simple.
Ps. 119:130

We speak of God's secret wisdom, a wisdom that has been hidden and that God destined for our glory before time began. None of the rulers of this age understood it.
I Cor. 2:7-8 NIV

We speak the wisdom of God in a mystery...that we might know the things...freely given to us by God. These things we also speak, not in words which man's wisdom teaches, but which the Holy Spirit teaches.... I Cor. 2:7,12-13

For the message about the Cross is foolishness to those who are perishing, but to us...it is the POWER OF GOD. I Cor. 1:18

For what other great nation has God so near...as the Lord our God when we call to Him? And what other great nation has statutes and ordinances as jus as this entire Law (The entire Bible!)? Deut. 4:7-8

It is God's will that by doing right you should silence the ignorance of the foolish.
I Pet. 2:15

Those who are wise shall shine like the brightness of the firmament and those who turn many to righteousness like the stars forever and ever. Dan. 12:3

Many shall be purified, cleansed, and refined, but the wicked shall continue to act wickedly. None of the wicked shall understand, but those who are wise shall understand.
Dan. 12:10

The wise among the people shall give understanding to many. Dan. 11:33

In the latter days you will understand it clearly. Jer. 23:20

We have not ceased praying for you and asking that you may be filled with the knowledge of God's will in all spiritual wisdom and understanding, so that you may lead lives worthy of the Lord, fully pleasing to Him. Col. 1:9-10

Prayer about the Wisdom of the Righteous

O Yeshua, our Redeemer, this generation has been raised on the foolishness of the world—of movies, cartoons, TV, video games, and secular music. We need help, Lord. Rescue us! I pray all Your people will abandon worldly wisdom, and will abide in Your Word, studying it and meditating on all of it until it sinks deep into their hearts and minds so the Holy Spirit can use it to make them wise. Yeshua, I pray people in this generation will seek to be mentored by those who are truly wise in Your wisdom—people who are taught and anointed by the Holy Spirit. I pray they will walk with the wise and learn from the wise until they, too, become wise (Prov. 13:20). Let there be multitudes upon multitudes of people who are wise in Your wisdom. And let them teach others so that the whole world becomes wise, so that stubborn foolishness disappears from the earth.

Thank You, Yeshua, that Your Word can make even the simple wise. Thank You that there is hope even for us who are the worst of fools. Thank You, Holy Spirit, that You teach us "*full insight and understanding in everything*" (II Tim. 2:7 AMP). Thank You that Your wisdom "*lifts us into the Glory of [Your] Presence*" (I Cor. 1:20). Praise be to Your Holy Name forever and ever. Amen.

Pray the Lord of the harvest to send out laborers. Matthew 9:39 NKJV

Persevere in supplication for all the saints. Ephesians 6:18

The Type of Leaders
We Need to Pray
for God to Send

Accursed is the one who is slack in doing the work of the Lord;
accursed is the one who keeps back the sword {the Word!} from
bloodshed {of satan's and his hosts' blood}. Jer. 48:10

Pray for God to send leaders today with John's purpose:

John was sent to "turn many...people...to the Lord their God...with...power...he will turn the hearts of parents to their children, and the disobedient to the wisdom of the righteous, to make ready a people prepared for the Lord." Lk. 1:16-17 (He must never drink wine or strong drink...he will be filled with the Holy Spirit, v. 15.)

Pray for True prophets who speak God's Word and turn people to the Lord:

Your prophets have seen for you false and deceptive visions; *they have not exposed your iniquity* to restore your fortunes, but have seen oracles for you that are false and misleading. Lam. 2:14

Thus says the Lord of hosts: do not listen to the words of the prophets who prophesy to you; they are deluding you. They speak visions of their own minds, not from the mouth of the Lord. They keep saying to those who despise the Word of the Lord, "It shall be well with you"; and to all who stubbornly follow their own stubborn hearts, they say, "No calamity shall come upon you." Jer. 23:16-17

My hand will be against the prophets who see false visions and utter lying divinations...[and] have misled my people, saying, "Peace," when there is no peace.
Ezek. 13:9,10

I did not send the prophets yet they ran; I did not speak to them yet they prophesied. But if they had stood in My council, then they would have proclaimed My Words to My people and they would have turned them from their evil way and from the evil of their doings.
Jer. 23:21-22

...[in] Christ we speak as persons of sincerity, as persons sent from God and standing in His presence. II Cor. 2:17

An appalling and horrible thing has happened in the land: the prophets prophesy falsely, and the priests rule as the prophets direct; My people love to have it so, but what will you do when the end comes? Jer. 5:30-31

Thus says the Lord concerning the prophets who lead My people astray.... Therefore it shall be night to you, without vision and darkness to you, without revelation. The sun shall go down upon the prophets, and the day shall be black over them; the seers shall be disgraced, and the diviners put to shame; they shall all cover their lips, for there is no answer from God. But as for me, I am filled with power, with the Spirit of the Lord. Micah 3:5-8

You shall speak My Word to them, whether they hear or refuse to hear; for they are a rebellious house. But you, mortal, hear what I say to you; do not be rebellious like that rebellious house; open your mouth and eat what I give you. I looked, and a hand was stretched out to me, and a written scroll was in it.... He said to me, O mortal, ...eat this scroll, and go, speak.... Eat this scroll...and fill your stomach with it. [KJV: Cause thy belly to eat, and fill thy bowels with this...that I give thee.] .... He said to me: Mortal, all My Words that I shall speak to you receive in your heart and hear with your ears; then go to the exiles, to your people, and speak to them. Ezek. 2:8-3:2,10-11

Let the one who has My Word speak My Word faithfully.... Is not My Word like fire, says the Lord, and like a hammer that breaks a rock in pieces? Jer. 23:28,29

Surely the Lord God does nothing, without revealing His secret to His servants the prophets. Amos 3:7

Ezra had set his heart to study the law of the Lord, and to do it, and to teach [it].
Ezra 7:10

Pray for sentinels who will blow the trumpet and give the warning:

If I bring the sword upon a land, and the people of the land take one of their number as their sentinel; and if the sentinel sees the sword coming upon the land and blows the trumpet and warns the people; then if any who hear the sound of the trumpet do not take warning...their blood shall be upon their own heads. But if they had taken warning, they would have saved their lives.... (cont.)

So you, mortal, I have made a sentinel for the house of Israel; whenever you hear a Word from My mouth, you shall give them warning from Me. If I say to the wicked, "O wicked ones, you shall surely die." And you do not speak to warn the wicked to turn from their ways, the wicked shall die in their iniquity, but their blood I will require at your hand. But if you warn the wicked to turn from their ways...you will have saved your life. Ezek. 33:2-9

Upon your walls, O Jerusalem, I have posted sentinels; all day and all night they shall never be silent. You who remind the Lord take no rest, and give Him no rest until He establishes Jerusalem and makes it renowned throughout the earth. Is. 62:6-7

Blow the trumpet in Zion; sound the alarm on My holy mountain! Joel 2:1

Blow the trumpet in Zion; sanctify a fast; call a solemn assembly; gather the people... the congregation; assemble the aged; ...the bridegroom...and the bride.... Joel 2:15-16

Sanctify a fast, call a solemn assembly. Gather the elders and all the inhabitants of the land to the house of the Lord your God, and cry out to the Lord. Alas for the day! For the day of the Lord is near, and as destruction from the Almighty it comes. Joel 1:14-15

Pray that the sentinels will always be listening:

To whom shall I speak and give warning, that they may hear? See, their ears are closed, they cannot listen. Jer. 6:10

Pray for Wise and True shepherds (Pray for the opposite of these verses.):

Mortal, prophesy against the shepherds...Ah, you shepherds...who have been feeding yourselves! Should not shepherds feed the sheep?... You have not strengthened the weak, you have not healed the sick, you have not bound up the injured, you have not brought back the strayed, you have not sought the lost, but with force and harshness you have ruled them. So they were scattered, ...and they became food for all the wild animals.... My sheep were scattered over all the face of the earth. Ezek. 34:1-5 (Read the whole chapter. There is judgment between sheep and sheep, too.)

And now, O priests, this command is for you. If you will not listen, if you will not lay it to heart to give glory to My Name, says the Lord of hosts, then I will send the curse on you and I will curse your blessings...and I will put you out of My presence. Mal. 2:1-2,3

Pray for Wise and True shepherds (Pray for the opposite of these verses.) (cont.)**:**

For the shepherds are stupid, and do not inquire of the Lord; therefore they have not prospered, and all their flock is scattered. Jer. 10:21

Pray for people to grieve:

The Lord called..., "Go through the city...and put a mark on the foreheads of those who sigh and groan over all the abominations that are committed in it." ...To others He said..., "Pass through the city after him, and kill; your eye shall not spare, and you shall show no pity...but touch no one who has the mark. And begin at My sanctuary." Ezek. 9:4-6

Alas for those who are at ease...who feel secure.... Alas for those who lie on beds of ivory, and lounge on their couches, who eat...who sing idle songs...and improvise on instruments of music; who drink wine from bowls, and anoint themselves with the finest oils, but are not grieved over the ruin of Joseph! Amos 6:4-6

Moan therefore, mortal; moan with breaking heart and bitter grief before their eyes. And when they say to you, "Why do you moan?" you shall say, "Because of the news that has come. Every heart will melt and all hands will be feeble, every spirit will faint and all knees will turn to water. See, it comes and it will be fulfilled," says the Lord God. Ezek. 21:6-7

Wail, you shepherds, and cry out; roll in ashes, you lords of the flock. Jer. 25:34

Let the priests, the ministers of the Lord, weep. Joel 2:17

...[L]ament, you priests; wail.... Come, pass the night in sackcloth, you ministers...! ...[C]all a solemn assembly. Gather the elders and all..., and cry out to the Lord. Joel 1:13,14

My eyes shed streams of tears because Your law is not kept. Ps. 119:136

Those who mourn are lifted to safety. Job 5:11

Woe to you who are laughing now, for you will mourn and weep. Lk. 6:25

When I heard this, I tore my garment and my mantle, and pulled hair from my head and beard, and sat appalled. Then all who trembled at the Words of the God of Israel, ...gathered around me.... Ezra...did not eat bread or drink water, for he was mourning over the faithlessness of the exiles. Ezra 9:3,4; 10:6

Pray for intercessors:

This is what the Lord God showed me: He was forming locusts at the time the latter growth began to sprout.... I said, "O Lord God, forgive, I beg you! How can Jacob stand: He is so small!" The Lord relented concerning this; "It shall not be," said the Lord..... The Lord God was calling for a shower of fire, and it devoured the great deep and was eating up the land. Then I said, "O Lord God, cease, I beg you! How can Jacob stand? He is so small!" The Lord relented concerning this; "This also shall not be," said the Lord God. Amos 7:1-6

[Moses speaking to the people] Then I lay prostrate before the Lord as before, forty days and forty nights; I neither ate bread nor drank water, because of all the sin you had committed, provoking the Lord by doing what was evil in His sight. For I was afraid that the anger that the Lord bore against you was so fierce that He would destroy you. But the Lord listened to me that time also. The Lord was so angry with Aaron that He was ready to destroy him, but I interceded also on behalf of Aaron at that same time. Deut. 9:16-20

[God speaking.] Shall I hide from Abraham what I am about to do? ...No.... (cont.)

[Abraham speaking to God.] Let me...speak to the Lord, I who am but dust and ashes.... Will You indeed sweep away the righteous with the wicked? ...Far be it from You! Shall not the Judge of all the earth do what is just? (cont.)

[God speaking] I will forgive the whole place for their sake.... Gen. 18:17-32

Pray for righteous people to intervene, so God will not have to destroy.

Run to and fro through the streets of Jerusalem, look around and take note! Search its squares and see if you can find ***one person*** who acts justly and seeks truth—so that I might pardon Jerusalem. Jer. 5:1

The Lord saw it, and it displeased Him...He saw that there was no one, and was appalled that there was no one to intervene. Is. 59:15-16

The people of the land have practiced extortion and committed robbery; they have oppressed the poor and needy.... And I sought for anyone among them who would repair the wall and stand in the breach before Me on behalf of the land, so that I would not destroy it; but I found no one. Therefore I have poured out My indignation upon them; I have consumed them with the fire of My wrath. Ezek. 22:29-31

He is always wrestling in his prayers on your behalf, so that you may stand mature and fully assured in everything that God wills. I testify for him that he has worked hard for you. Col. 4:12

Pray for leaders of purity and integrity:

I will walk with integrity of heart within my house; I will not set before my eyes anything that is base [Hebrew dictionary: worthless, destructive, wicked, evil, ungodly]. I hate the work of those who fall away; it shall not cling to me. Perverseness of heart shall be far from me; I will know nothing of evil. Ps. 101:2-4

Those who walk righteously and speak uprightly...who stop their ears from hearing of bloodshed and shut their eyes from looking on evil, they will live on the heights....
Is. 33:14-16

In amazement the whole earth followed the beast.... The beast was given a mouth uttering haughty and blasphemous words.... It opened its mouth to utter blasphemies against God, blaspheming His Name and His dwelling.... It was given authority over every tribe and people and language and nation, and all the inhabitants of the earth will worship it.... It deceives the inhabitants of earth.... It was allowed to give breath to the image of the beast so that the image...could even speak. Rev. 13:3, 5-6,14-15

I have a question. Is it possible that this prophecy is partially being fulfilled today? Are not today's songs, movies, and TV shows full of blasphemy to the Lord, dragging His Name and honor in the dirt? Do they not ridicule the pure things of God, and glorify immorality? Does not the whole world sit and stare at the screens, or listen to their ipods by the hour? Would it not be considered worship if we gave that much time and attention to Jesus and His Word? Is not the whole world, especially all the young people (even the Believing ones), being influenced and, dare I say, deceived, by this industry?

Pray for leaders of purity and integrity (cont.)**:**

The light of the body is the eye. Matt. 6:22 KJV

Cast away the detestable things your eyes feast on, every one of you, and do not defile yourselves...I am the Lord your God.... But none of them cast away the detestable things their eyes feasted on.... Then I thought I would pour out My wrath upon them and spend My anger against them.... Will you defile yourselves...and go astray after their detestable things? As I live, says the Lord God, I will not be consulted by you.

Ezek. 20:7-8,31

All...who took pleasure in unrighteousness will be condemned. II Thess. 2:12

Are not those who find pleasure in watching evil just as guilty as those who partake? Were not the Roman citizens just as guilty for watching the Believers being killed by lions as the leaders in charge of it? Are we better than the Romans because what we watch is just acting? But is it really just pretend? The ones who climb in bed together on screen, are they not doing the same kinds of things off screen? Are not the half-truths, false beliefs, and degrading humor spoken on screen absorbed by young people and immediately mimicked off screen, changing the culture of each generation? Has not the screen's atmosphere that respects nothing as sacred, leaked out into the customs of our day? So how can we say it's just acting, and therefore we have no guilt? Besides, if we get pleasure from watching unrighteousness, what does that say about the inside of our hearts?

I know the things that come into your mind. Ezek. 11:5

[They] have profaned My holy things; they have made no distinction between the holy and the common, ...between the unclean and the clean, ...so that I am profaned among them. Ezek. 22:26

For this reason God sends them a powerful delusion, leading them to believe what is false. II Thess. 2:11

First clean the inside so the outside also may become clean. Matt. 23:26:

You may say, "The things I watch aren't so bad." In response to that, I challenge you to try a year without the media: no TV, no cartoons, no movies, no games, no secular books or music, etc. Spend your time soaking only in the presence of Jesus, and in His Word, letting it change you and make you wise. Then see if you are not shocked by what is on the screen.

After people fast the media for long periods, usually when they return to the screen they are shocked by what they see. They can't believe that the things they used to think were innocent are actually very much against God's Word and God's Truth!! It grieves them and causes them to cry out to God for mercy for this generation. (If you add forty days of water-only-fasting-and-praying onto the media fast, the affect is nothing short of spectacular.)

It is like people who live in a foul-smelling place so long their noses don't detect it anymore. They would say their place doesn't stink. But take them out of it to fresh air for awhile, and when they return, they are repulsed by the filthy stench.

I have been around people whose calling is deliverance ministry. They say they cannot watch TV or movies because it causes them to lose their anointing power in the Holy Spirit. They say they must keep their minds pure, constantly staying focused on God, and praying in the Spirit, to protect the anointing.

So what are we losing in our relationship with the Lord when we feast our eyes and ears on the immorality of the media? Why would we do anything that could possibly hinder that relationship or the flow of the Holy Spirit's power in our lives? When I've watched things that did not bring glory to Jesus, I've found that it took away my sense of closeness to Him. Why would I let anything separate me from Him even for a minute? Father, forgive me.

Do not quench the Spirit. I Thess. 5:19

Do not grieve the Holy Spirit of God. Eph. 4:30

[Jesus] said to them, "...for what is prized by human beings is an abomination in the sight of God." Lk. 16:15

O Jesus, forgive us! Purify our desires until media filth becomes "an abomination" to *us,* too. I thank you, Jesus, for all the young people who *are* allowing You to purify them. Thank you for parents and youth leaders like Lou Engle who are inspiring young people by the 1000's. Let there be more, Jesus, more and more from all ages—from preteens to the elderly—who set themselves apart for You.

And Lord, may the people to whom You have given the exceptional talents for this business cleanse themselves and offer all their skills to You for the honorable work of Your Kingdom. Help them to make great movies that speak Your deep, profound truths; movies that grip the viewers; movies that make them hungry for more; movies that cause them to ponder until the message sinks into their beliefs; movies so powerful that they turn people's hearts to YOU, Jesus!

And may the desire in people to watch immorality, and the money coming in for the filth dry up completely! In Your Holy Name, JESUS, THE MESSIAH!!

Whoever cleanses himself...who separates himself from contact with contaminating and corrupting influences, will...be a vessel set apart and useful for honorable and noble purposes, consecrated and profitable to the Master, fit and ready for any good work.

II Tim. 2:7 AMP

"Through those who are near Me I will show Myself holy, and before all the people I will be glorified." Lev. 10:3

Pray for leaders to whom furthering God's Kingdom is more important than life itself:

They overcame [the enemy] by the Blood of the Lamb and by the Word [in] their testimony, and they did not love their lives to the death. Rev. 12:11 NKJV

There are many such leaders still today in China, Laos, Africa, the Middle East, and other places, who are doing just that—risking their lives for the Gospel. Many are being tortured and even killed. I have the awesome privilege of knowing one of them who has suffered and yet still continues to risk her life for Jesus. I am amazed by her courage.

O Lord, bless them. May they receive the highest rewards in Your Kingdom. Protect the ones still living, Jesus. Put legions of angels around them. Break prison doors for them and cut through bars of iron (Is. 45:2). Blind the eyes of their enemies. Do mighty miracles.

Magnify their light, Lord. Let even their captors and persecutors be touched and changed by their testimony. Give them abundant harvest of souls everywhere they go, even their fellow prisoners. We thank you for them, Jesus. Bless them with every spiritual blessing, and every other kind of blessing. In Your powerful Name.

Prayers for Leaders

Sept. 29, '05 (On Jeremiah 23)

O Jesus, I pray the prophets will stand in Your council and will not go out until You send them with Your POWERFUL, MIGHTY WORDS, that really do turn people from their wickedness!!!

O Jesus, call prophets that will stand in both Your council and counsel for days and days, and weeks and weeks, and years and years, and will NOT move until You clothe them with POWER from on High and You send them out.

I pray Your prophets will sit at Your feet and listen. I pray they are right now listening and listening, and drinking in Your Word, taking it into their hearts and repenting. I pray they are eating Your Word like You told Ezekiel to do; eating it even though it is bitter (like it was for John in Revelations); taking it into their bowels—their inner soul, letting it do YOUR WORK in their hearts.

I pray this for your prophets, your missionaries, your pastors, your teachers, your senators, your talk show hosts, your leaders....

May they stay in Your presence
Repenting, repenting, repenting...
Listening, listening, listening...
Pondering, pondering, pondering...
Learning, learning, learning...
Changing, changing, changing...
Becoming wiser and wiser and wiser...
Until they are FULL OF ONLY YOUR wisdom
And empty of man's wisdom.

Then send them in Your confidence and boldness, bearing Your TRUE WISDOM. Send them to strategic places where Your MIGHTY WORD will have the MOST POWERFUL, far-reaching affect.

Send them with Your WORD that is like FIRE and like a HAMMER that breaks a rock in pieces!!!

Thank You for the ones You are sending, Jesus. And thank You for the ones You have sent already.

Nov. 3, '05

In Christ we speak as persons of sincerity, as persons sent from God and standing in His presence. II Cor. 2:17

Jesus, I pray again for You to cause Your leaders to stand in Your presence and soak in Your Word and be fed constantly by Your Word, not by movies or TV or video games or anything else—only Your Word, so they are *in* You, waiting until You send them and You speak Your Word to Your people through them. Let Your Word be spoken and revealed by people of sincerity who are *in* You and sent by You.

Let there be more and more—multitudes upon multitudes of people—leaders who are *in* You, standing in Your presence, feeding on Your Word so they can speak Your Words and cause people, through the Holy Spirit, to hear Your Word and turn from evil, turn completely away from evil, to holiness in You, Jesus—to You who art Holy, Holy, Holy. Let there be more leaders whom You purify and anoint with Your resurrection power.

November years back

O Jesus, I'm haunted by the fact that people on some mission teams know more about all the latest movies than they do about Your Word. They talk about movies and cartoons, and joke about the morbid, almost vulgar stuff in them more than they talk about You and Scripture. They hardly ever talk about the Bible except at designated "spiritual" times. The abundance of their hearts is movies and cartoons. I am mourning and grieving in lamentation.

They pray wonderful Spirit-filled prayers one moment, then joke about very sacrilegious things the next, dragging the sacred into the gutter of unseemly humor. *From the same mouth come blessing and cursing. My brothers and sisters, this ought not to be so* (James 3:10). Out of the same mouths come "spiritual" talk and prayer, and then tainted humor. This ought not be.

It saddens me. I am tortured by it. How does it make You feel, Jesus? They talked about having learned "grace." Does "grace" mean we can get our pleasure from watching sin in the movies; our humor from joking about sin the way they do in the movies; and our beauty from wearing the latest revealing fashions they wear in the movies? Is that what "grace" and "freedom in Christ" mean, Jesus?

You prayed, Jesus, that we be one as You and the Father are one. The mission teams are "one" by way of movies and cartoons, but also seem to be "one" when they pray. Is that okay with You, Jesus?

[After crying out to Jesus like this, each mission trip I went on was more spiritually pure than the one before. On the best one the people talked about God and the Bible all the time. They were full of Holy Spirit power. They spent all their spare time either reading Scripture to bless each other, or singing and praying and crying out to Jesus together. They purposely didn't watch things on TV so as to keep their hearts and minds pure and sensitive to the Holy Spirit. It was so refreshing and wonderful, I felt like I was in heaven!! And the power of God moved in that team's ministry. We saw many people set free from the enemy's bondage. Praise the Lord!! Thank You, Jesus!]

Jan. 27, '06

From the days of John the Baptist until now the kingdom of heaven has suffered violence [note: *has been coming violently*] *and the violent take it by force. For all the prophets and the Law prophesied until John came.* Matt. 11:12-13

Yes, it has been through much persecution and bloodshed that the Kingdom of God has been coming! Even martyrs' blood still today! And most of all Jesus' pure, all-powerful Blood.

O Jesus, help us to take Your Kingdom by force. Help us to fight for Your kingdom!!! Help us to be courageous and have no fear, not even a smidgen of the fear of man, or the fear of failure, or of anything!

May 12, '06

It was given authority over every tribe and people and language and nation, and all the inhabitants of the earth will worship it, everyone whose name has not been written...in the book of life of the Lamb. Rev. 13:7-8

Jesus, I have a question. Who gave the beast this authority? It couldn't be You, because You gave us "authority over ALL the power of the enemy" (Lk. 10:9). So it must be us. We must have relinquished our authority and given it to him. O Jesus, forgive us! Help us to take it back from him! Help us to step into our position of loosing and binding (Matt. 16:19). Help us to bind him in chains and banish him from the earth, and to loose all the people from his bonds of deception and set them free so their blind eyes can be opened to see You for who You are and worship You.

Mar. 3, '03 (Pray this prayer for yourself as a leader.)

I have food to eat that you do not know about.... My food is to do the will of Him who sent Me and to complete His work.... I tell you, look around you, and see how the fields are ripe for harvesting. The reaper is already receiving wages and is gathering fruit for eternal life so that the sower and reaper may rejoice together. Jn. 4:32,34,35-36

O Jesus, I want this to be my food, too!! This needs to be my food: –to do the will of **You** who sent me! –to complete Your work!! –and to gather fruit for eternal life!!! (Let me repeat this to myself.)

My food is to do Your will.
My food is to complete the work You gave me.
My food is to gather fruit for ETERNAL LIFE!!!
My food is to please the Holy Spirit.

My food is to cause the Holy Spirit to rejoice (not to grieve!).

–to (the opposite of "quench"...um..."fuel!") to be fuel to the Holy Spirit in me!

–to be an opening or a furnace for the Holy Spirit's FIRE!!! (instead of being a fire-wall that stops the fire or something that quenches the fire!)

Yes, Lord Jesus, change me. Change the material I'm made of from quenching material to combustible material—from dust to (...um...) oil!!! Wash away all my dust and dirt and ashes with Your *washing of water by the Word* (Eph. 5:26) so I can be filled with the oil of the Holy Spirit so the Holy Spirit's FIRE will burn continually in me!

For what is prized by humans is an abomination to God. Lk. 16:15

Almost all the TV shows I flicked through last night on the hotel cable TV were completely an abomination. So, I must give up TV and movies completely to help get rid of all my ashes and dirt, right, Jesus?

Sept 18 and Oct. 15, '05

O Lord and Savior, Jesus Christ, I pray please bring more Josephs into the world to live pure lives; to be wise in Your Word and to interpret things *correctly*; to follow You and live for You no matter how terrible the setting, no matter how severe the temptations; to allow You to strengthen them and prepare them to be ready for their high callings when it is their moment. I pray for many Josephs, Daniels, Davids, Stephens, Peters, Philips, Pauls, Johns, Esthers, Ruths, Annas, and Marys. May they be *blameless and innocent children of* [You] *without blemish in the midst of* [this] *crooked and perverse generation...*[and] *shine as...*[lights] *in the world* (Phil. 2:15-16). And may they take back this world from the enemy!

We...will devote ourselves to prayer. Acts 6:3

Releasing Funds
for God's Kingdom Work

He said to them, "Take nothing for your journey, no staff, nor bag, nor bread, nor money—not even an extra tunic. Lk. 9:3

"You received without payment; give without payment. Take no gold, or silver, or copper in your belts, no bag for your journey, or two tunics, or sandals, or a staff; for laborers deserve their food." Mt. 10:9

"Carry no purse." Lk. 10:4

He said to them, "When I sent you out without a purse, bag, or sandals, did you lack anything?" They said, "No, not a thing." Lk. 22:35

"Strive first for the Kingdom of God and His righteousness, and all these things will be given to you as well." Matt. 6:33

In the same way, the Lord commanded that those who proclaim the Gospel should get their living by the Gospel. I Cor. 9:14

"It is not right that we should neglect the Word of God in order to ... [raise funds?]....
We, for our part, will devote ourselves to prayer and to serving the Word." Acts 6:2-3

I have been young, and now am old, yet I have not [NIV: never] seen the righteous forsaken or their children begging bread. They are ever giving liberally and lending and their children become a blessing. Ps. 37:25-26

For which of you, intending to build a tower, does not first sit down and estimate the cost, to see whether he has enough to complete it? ...Or what king, going out to war against another king, will not sit down first and consider...? Lk. 14:28,31
I'm sure God did what Jesus advises here. I'm sure He sat down and counted the cost of completing His Kingdom and defeating His enemy. He has enough funds and supplies and soldiers to finish the mission!! Let's pray for the release of it all.

How can one enter a strong man's house and plunder his property, without first tying up the strong man? Then indeed the house can be plundered. Matt. 12:29 [Jesus has bound up the strong man. Let's pray now for the plundering both in souls and in finances.]

For to the one who pleases Him God gives wisdom and knowledge and joy; but to the sinner He gives the work of gathering and heaping, only to give to one who pleases God.
Ecc. 2:26

The sinner's wealth is laid up for the righteous. Prov. 13:22
The abundance of the sea shall be brought to you. Is. 60:5
Nations shall bring you their wealth. Is. 60:11
The wealth of the nations shall come to you. Is. 60:5
I will extend...the wealth of the nations like an overflowing stream. Is. 66:12

You shall be named ministers of our God; you shall enjoy the wealth of the nations....
All who see shall acknowledge that [you] are a people whom the Lord has blessed.
Is. 61:6,9

God provided even through heathen kings and people!

The Lord had filled them with joy by changing the attitude of the king..., so that he assisted them in the work on the house of God. Ezra 6:22 NIV

The king's heart is a stream of water in the hand of the Lord; He turns it wherever He will. Prov. 21:1

In order that the Word of the Lord by the mouth of Jeremiah might be accomplished, the Lord stirred up the spirit of **King** Cyrus **of Persia** so that he sent a herald throughout all his kingdom, and also in a written edict declared: "Thus says King Cyrus of Persia: The Lord, the God of heaven, has given me all the kingdoms of the earth, and He has charged me to build Him a house at Jerusalem in Judah. ...His people—may their God be with them!—are now permitted to go up to Jerusalem in Judah, and rebuild the house of the Lord...; and let all...be assisted...with **silver and gold**, with **goods** and with animals, besides **freewill offerings** for the house of God in Jerusalem." (cont.)

...Everyone whose spirit God had stirred—got ready to go up and rebuild the house of the Lord in Jerusalem. All their neighbors aided them with **silver** vessels, with **gold**, with **goods**, with animals, and with **valuable gifts**, besides all that was **freely offered**. Ezra 1:1-11

King Cyrus issued a decree: Concerning the house of God at Jerusalem, let the house be rebuilt...; ...**let the cost be paid from the royal treasury.** Ezra 6:3-5

As soon as they came to the house of the Lord in Jerusalem, some of the heads of families made freewill offerings for the house of God, to erect it on its site. According to their resources they gave to the building fund sixty-one thousand darics of **gold**, five thousand minas of **silver**, and one hundred priestly robes. Ezra 2:68-69

So they gave **money** to the masons and the carpenters, and food, drink, and...cedar trees from Lebanon to the sea, to Joppa, according to the grant that they had from King Cyrus of Persia. Ezra 3:7

Now you, Tettenai, governor, ...keep away; let the work on this house of God alone; let the governor of the Jews and the elders of the Jews rebuild this house of God on its site. ...The cost is to be paid to these people, in full and without delay, from the royal revenue.... Whatever is needed—young bulls, rams, or sheep for burnt offerings to the God of heaven, wheat, salt, wine, or oil, as the priests in Jerusalem require—let that be given to them day by day without fail, so that they may offer pleasing sacrifices to the God of heaven, and pray for the life of the king and his children.... I, Darius, make a decree; let it be done with all diligence." Ezra 5:6-12

Ezra went up from Babylonia. He was a scribe skilled in the law of Moses that the Lord the God of Israel had given; and **the king granted him all that he asked**, for the hand of the Lord his God was upon him.... For Ezra had set his heart to study the law of the Lord, and to do it, and to teach the statutes and ordinances in Israel. Ezra 7:6,10

This is a copy of the letter... : Artaxerxes, King of kings to the priest Ezra, the scribe of the law of the God of heaven; Peace.... For you are sent by the king... to convey the **silver and gold that the king and his counselors have freely offered** to the God of Israel...with **all the silver and gold** that you shall find **in the whole province of Babylonia**, and with the freewill offerings of the people and the priests.... **And whatever else is required** for the house of your God, which you are responsible for providing, **you may provide out of the king's treasury.** Ezra 7:11-20

I, King Artaxerxes, decree to all the treasurers in the province Beyond the River: whatever the priest Ezra, the scribe of the law of the God of heaven, requires of you, let it be done with all diligence.... Ezra 7:21

Then I said to the king, "If it pleases the king, let letters be given me to the governors of the province Beyond the River, that they may grant me passage until I arrive in Judah; and a letter to Asaph, the keeper of the king's forest, directing him to give me timber to make beams for the gates of the temple fortress, and for the wall of the city, and for the house that I shall occupy." **And the king granted me what I asked**, for the gracious hand of my God was upon me. Neh. 2:7-8

So the elders of the Jews built and prospered, through the prophesying of the prophet, Haggai and Zechariah, son of Iddo. They finished their building by command of the God of Israel and by decree of Cyrus, Darius, and King Artaxerxes of Persia. Ezra 6:14-15

The Egyptians urged the people to hasten their departure from the land, for they said, "We shall all be dead."...The Israelites had done as Moses told them; they had asked the Egyptians for jewelry of silver and gold, and for clothing, and the Lord had given the people favor in the sight of the Egyptians, so that **they let them have what they asked**. And so they plundered the Egyptians. Ex. 12:33, 35-36

The Israelites later offered those Egyptian gifts for the building of the tabernacle.

And they came, everyone whose heart was stirred, and everyone whose spirit was willing, and brought the Lord's offering to be used for the tent of meeting, and for all its service, and for the sacred vestments. So they came, both men and women; all who were of a willing heart.... And the leaders brought onyx stones and gems to be set in the ephod and the breastpiece.... All the Israelite men and women whose hearts made them willing to bring anything for the work that the Lord had commanded by Moses to be done, brought it as a freewill offering to the Lord. Ex. 35:21-24, 27-29

God can even lay it on a heathen king's heart to provide for the teaching of God's Word.

"And you, Ezra, according to the God-given wisdom you possess, appoint magistrates and judges who may judge all the people in the province Beyond the River who know the laws of your God; and you shall teach those who do not know them." Ezra 7:25-26

Blessed be the Lord, the God of our ancestors, who put such a thing as this into the heart of the king to glorify the house of the Lord in Jerusalem. Ezra 7:27 (Yes, indeed! Praise be to God!)

Prayer for Releasing Funds

Mar. 9, '06

My thoughts today are on fund-raising. Some organizations even give seminars on how to raise funds. It's a whole culture. They have to spend months making call after call, going to church after church until they are weary! I feel so sorry for them!

Yeshua, we don't see You ever asking for money. Yet You had enough that You gave to the poor. (At the Last Supper, the disciples thought Judas was leaving to go give money to the poor, as if that was normal.) And Judas was managing Your finances. So You had enough money to need a manager. You also had enough that You needed to pay taxes, which you got from the mouth of a fish!

You provided for Your disciples through miraculous catches of fish where there had been no fish. It was so much it almost broke their nets. You lived with Peter, and You gave his family great medical care and insurance, namely, healing! You were so rich You could feed 4000 and 5000 people until they were full and had lots of leftovers!

O Yeshua Adonai, let that kind of abundance, and miraculous supply come to Your hard-working Kingdom laborers. Help them to believe and trust in Your provision and Your miracles, and let them begin to see those miracles every day.

Thank you for the ones who already know You as their miracle working Jehovah Jirah. (I think of Rolland and Heidi Baker of Iris Ministries, for example.) Thank You for their marvelous testimonies. Continue to bless them overwhelmingly. Let all who proclaim the Gospel get their living by the Gospel! (I Cor. 9:14)

Mar. 11, '06

The Lord told me last night that the reason He is letting me see this missionary culture of fund-raising is *not* so I can get discouraged. It is so I will pray. So I am praying.

Mar. 13, '06

O Yeshua, I pray that what You caused to happen in Nehemiah and Ezra's day will begin to happen today. Turn the hearts of kings and rulers, and millionaires and billionaires toward Your work. Lay it on their hearts to give freely and abundantly to Your people who are carrying out Your great commission.

Take the wealth from the secular world, Yeshua, and release it into Your Kingdom work. Let there be abundant flow to all those called by Your Name who are doing Your work. Release abundance to them. Give them all the funds they need, Yeshua, so they can move forward in Your work, so they do not have to spend any of their time in fund raising, so they do not have to beg. Yeshua, let us, like David, never again see Your righteous people begging (Ps. 37:25).

I speak to the enemy that he must release his hold on the wealth of the world. It is not his. It does not belong to him. He must take his hands off of all of it and leave it alone in Jesus Name, by the Power of the Blood of Jesus.

In the Power of the Name of Jesus, and by the authority of that Name, I go into the spiritual realm and I snatch the wealth out of the kingdom of darkness and release it into the Kingdom of Light.

I ask You, God, to open the floodgates of the windows of heaven and release a flow that is so abundant that it cannot be contained. And I bind in chains the enemy who is blocking that flow, and I speak to him to be removed and cast into the Lake of Fire, in Your Holy Name, Jesus.

Jesus, let the wealth of the secular world flow to all Your marvelous work going on in this world today:

to Campus Crusade and all its branches, including The JESUS Film Project and the International School Project, and to all their individual missionaries, including all the teachers in Mongolia, and Eric and Alison Foster ministering in India and Africa; to the International House of Prayer (IHOP) and all its subdivisions and prayer missionaries, including Justice House of Prayer (JHOP), The Cause USA, The Call, Bound4Life, Facedown 40, Uprising, Rumble University, and The Elijah Revolution;

to all the Billy Graham and Franklin Graham organizations, including The Samaritan's Purse; to the 700 Club and all its international organizations and outreaches; to Joyce Meyers and all the marvelous works being done through her organizations;

to Wycliff, to the Mercy Ships, to Bruce Wilson's work, including Dream Africa; to all youth ministries, including One Day, YWAM and the Joshua Revolution; to all the Bible Colleges that are teaching Your Truth, including Christ for the Nations and Elim Bible Institute;

to all Christian publishers, especially small ones like Elim Publishing; to all great Christian discipleship writers like John Bevere, Francis Frangipane, Bob Sorge, Beth Moore and many more;

to all the people You have sent to work in Israel and the Middle East; to all Messianic Jewish congregations, to all who are evangelizing and praying for the Jewish communities around the world: Jews for Jesus, Watchman on the Wall, Rabbi Jim Appel and his congregation, and the more and more thousands of others being called to this every day;

to all missionary organizations working all over the world, including, House of God, New Tribes Missions, YWAM, Helimission, Elim Fellowship and to all individual missionaries, including the ones I know: the Tobin's in Laos, the Greenawalt's in Hungary, the Cadles' in China, Miss Keplinger in Mexico, the Good's working in Africa and America; and many others whose names are too numerous to fit here;

to all Your pastors and true churches, and to all church planters including my long time friends, the Eby's;

to all the Christian orphanages around the world, including, Ishmael Tribal Mission in India, the Agape Home for orphans with AIDS in Thailand, and the Hope Foster Home and others in China;

to all Your churches in China, and to all the mission work being sent out from there and from all other countries in Asia, Africa, Europe, Central and South America, Australia, India, Canada and the Middle East.

Lord, You know all of them, all their organizations' names, and all the names of all the individual workers. Bless them and provide for them all, Jesus.

Release the funds, Jesus. Lay it on the hearts of all the rich, as You laid it on the hearts of Kings Cyrus, Darius, Artexerxes, and on the Egyptians to give to Your people and Your work. Let the hearts of all the wealthy and all those in control of money be like streams of water in Your hand to turn them where You will. You told King Cyrus that he was supposed to build Your house. Lay it on the rich and powerful people now that they are supposed to build Your house today—Your house made of living stones.

Thank You that You have already done this to an extent in Russia and Mongolia. There You have laid it on the leaders' and rulers' hearts to open the doors and invite Your Word to be taught in their schools. THANK YOU! THANK YOU!

And thank You that You have laid it on the hearts of the Chinese leaders to open their doors for English teachers and business people to come and teach and do business in their country, thus opening a way for Your Kingdom people to get in. THANK YOU! THANK YOU!

Keep opening more doors, and keep providing abundant, overflowing funds, Jesus, so people can keep walking through those open doors.

Release the wealth of the nations, Jesus. Release the wealth of all the international companies. Release the wealth of all the Fortune 500 companies. Release the wealth of all the famous sports players and the owners and managers, and all the successful actors and actresses and movie industry people. Release it all—all the secular and Christian wealth of the world into Your Kingdom, into fulfilling Your Great Commission, Jesus, into taking the Gospel to the ends of the earth, into preaching the Gospel to every creature, and into making disciples of all nations. Release all the funds needed. Release an overwhelming flow so Your work may be done and Your Commission completed, so You may return to the earth and take us all home.

COME LORD JESUS!

[I was praying this way at a powerful prayer meeting. The Lord had just pointed out the Scriptures in Ezra to me that morning. An African lady was beside me who was in desperate need of funds for her Christian work. Many people had been praying for her. Right after that meeting she was given a totally unexpected very huge amount of money. It really built my faith! May it strengthen yours, too.]

Mar. 21, '06

Worthy is the Lamb that was slaughtered to receive power and **wealth***...* (Rev. 12:5). Wealth! Yes, Jesus! That's what I'm praying for! May You receive all the POWER of the universe, and all the WEALTH of the world! May Your Kingdom receive all the wealth of the universe. You are worthy, and it all belongs to You. May it all be loosed from where it is and be brought into Your Kingdom.

But see, we are slaves today.... Because of our sins, [our] abundant harvest goes to the kings You have placed over us. They rule over our bodies...as they please. We are in great distress (Neh. 9:36-37 NIV). O Jesus, many people feel this way today—enslaved to their jobs. But let this not be the reason Your workers are short on funds. Let it not be so for Your Kingdom workers. Set them free, Jesus. Set us all free from our sins and from bondage. Thank You, Jesus. You are all about freedom!

You who remind the Lord, take no rest and give Him no rest until He establishes Jerusalem and makes it renown throughout the earth.

Isaiah 62:7

My heart's desire and prayer to God for [Israel] is that they be saved.

Romans 10:12

Prophesies for Israel and Jerusalem That Have Not Yet Been Fulfilled

The Jews are God's Special People and They Shall All Be Saved

Then what advantage has the Jew? Or what is the value of circumcision? **Much in every way**. Rom. 3:1

As regarding election, they are **beloved**. For the gifts and callings of God are irrevocable. Rom. 11:28-29

You who remind the Lord, take no rest, and give Him no rest until He establishes Jerusalem and makes it **renown** throughout the earth. Is. 62:7

I have great sorrow and unceasing anguish in my heart...for...my own people.... They are Israelites and **to them belong** the adoption, the glory, the covenants, the giving of the Law, the worship and the promises...the patriarchs and from them...comes the Messiah who is over all, God blessed forever, Amen. Rom. 9:1-4

My heart's desire and prayer to God for them [Israel] is that they be saved. I can testify that they have a zeal for God but it is not enlightened. Rom. 10:1-2

As regard the Gospel they are enemies of God **for your sake**.... They have now... been disobedient **in order that** by mercy shown to you, they too may now...receive mercy. For God has imprisoned all in disobedience so that He may be merciful to all. O the depth of the riches and wisdom...of God! Rom. 11:28-34

For on My Holy mountain, the mountain height of Israel, says the Lord God, there all the house of Israel, all of them, shall serve Me in the land.... Ezek. 20:40

If their stumbling means **riches** for the world...how much more will their **full inclusion** mean [to the world]! ...If their rejection is **reconciliation** of the world, what will their **acceptance** be but **life from the dead** [for the world]! Rom. 11:12,15

When?

So that you may not claim to be wiser than you are...understand this mystery: a hardening has come upon **part** of Israel until the **full** number of the Gentiles has come in. And so **all Israel will be saved**. Rom. 11:25-26

And Jerusalem will be trampled on by the Gentiles, until the times of the Gentiles are fulfilled. Lk. 21:24

...until **the full number of the Gentiles has come in**. Rom. 11:25

...it has been given to the Gentiles. They will trample the holy city for 42 months. Rev. 11:2 NIV

He shall make sacrifice and offering cease; and in their place shall be an abomination that desolates, until the decreed end is poured out upon the desolator. Dan. 9:27

The end will come like a flood: war will continue until the end, and desolations have been decreed. Dan. 9:26 NIV

One of them said..., "How long shall it be until the end....?" ...And I heard him swear by the One who lives forever that...when the **shattering of the power of the holy people comes to an end**, all these things would be accomplished. Dan. 12:6-7

Jerusalem, Jerusalem.... How often have I desired to gather your children together as a hen gathers her brood under her wings and you were not willing. See, your house is left to you desolate. For I tell you, **you will not see me again until you say, "Blessed is the One who comes in the Name of the Lord."** Matt. 23:37-39

But You O Lord...will rise up and have compassion on Zion for it is time to favor it; the appointed time has come. For Your servants **hold its stones dear** and **have pity on its dust**. {If you go to Israel, these words will have special significance to you, because that's mostly what the land around Jerusalem is, dust and stones!} The nations will fear the Name of the Lord and all the kings of the earth Your Glory. For the Lord will build up Zion; He will appear in His Glory. Ps. 102:12-17

Alas! That day is so great there is none like it; it is a time of distress for Jacob [most likely the Holocaust]; yet he shall be rescued from it. On that day, says the Lord of hosts, I will break the yoke from off his neck, and I will burst his bonds, and strangers shall no more make a servant of him. But they will serve the Lord their God.... Jer. 30:7-9

My Holy Name I will make known among My people Israel; and I will not let My Holy Name be profaned any more; and the nations shall know that I am the Lord, the Holy One in Israel. It has come! It has happened, says the Lord God. This is the day of which I have spoken. Ezek. 39:7-8

Israel's Repentance
(This is not meant to be singling out Jewish people as sinners. We are all sinners.)

Thus says the Lord God; It is not for your sake, O house of Israel, that I am about to act, but for the sake of My Holy Name, which you have profaned among the nations to which you came. I will sanctify My great Name, ... and the nations shall know that I am the Lord, says the Lord God, when through you I display My holiness before their eyes...I will sprinkle clean water upon you, and you shall be clean.... A new heart I will give you, and a new spirit I will put within you.... Then you shall remember your evil ways, and your dealings that were not good; and you shall loathe yourselves.... Ezek. 36:22-31

There you shall remember your ways and all the deeds by which you have polluted yourselves; and you shall loathe yourselves for all the evils that you have committed. And you shall know that I am the Lord, when I deal with you for My Name's sake, not according to your evil ways, or corrupt deeds, O house of Israel, says the Lord God. Ezek. 20:43-44

[Moses to the Israelites] From there [in the disbursement] you will seek the Lord your God and you will find Him if you seek after Him with all your heart and soul. Deut. 4:29

In your distress, when all these things have happened to you in the time to come, you will return to the Lord your God and heed Him. Deut. 4:30

They shall come weeping as they seek the Lord their God. They shall ask the way to Zion, with faces turned toward it, and they shall come and join themselves to the Lord by an everlasting covenant that shall never be forgotten. Jer. 50:5

Penalty is Paid

As a mother comforts her child, so I will comfort you; you shall be comforted in Jerusalem. Is. 66:13

Comfort, O comfort My people, says your God. Speak tenderly to Jerusalem, and cry to her that she has served her term, that her penalty is paid, that she has received from the Lord's hand double for all her sins. Is. 40:1-2

The light of the moon will be like the light of the sun, and the light of the sun will be sevenfold, like the light of seven days, on the day when the Lord binds up the injuries of His people and heals the wounds inflicted by His blow. Is. 30:26

Penalty is Paid (cont.)

Surely He has borne our griefs and carried our sorrows...He was wounded for our transgressions, He was bruised for our iniquities; The chastisement for our peace was upon Him, and by His stripes we are healed.... And the Lord has laid on Him the iniquity of us all.... He was led as a Lamb to the slaughter.... He poured out His soul unto death.

Is. 53:4-5,7,12

The Jews were entrusted with the oracles of God. What if some were unfaithful? Will their faithlessness nullify the faithfulness of God? **By no means!** Rom. 3:1

I will heal your faithlessness. Jer. 3:22

On that day a fountain shall be opened for the house of David and the inhabitants of Jerusalem, to cleanse them from sin and impurity.... They will call on My Name, and I will answer them. I will say, "They are My people"; and they will say, "The Lord is our God."

Zech. 13:1,9

In those days and at that time, says the Lord, the iniquity of Israel shall be sought, and there shall be none; and the sins of Judah and none shall be found; for I will pardon the remnant that I spared. Jer. 50:20

I will restore them because I have compassion on them. They will be as though I had not rejected them, for I am the Lord their God. Zech. 10:6 NIV

They shall seek refuge in the Name of the Lord—the remnant of Israel; they shall do no wrong and utter no lies, nor shall a deceitful tongue be found in their mouths.

Zeph. 3:12-13

The Ingathering (This has been happening since 1947)

They will come together from the lands in the north to the land I gave your ancestors as their heritage. Jer. 3:18 NIV

I will save My people from the countries of the east and the west. I will bring them back to live in Jerusalem. Zech. 8:7-8

I will bring Israel back to its own pasture. Jer. 50:19 NIV

Do not be dismayed, O Israel; for I am going to save you from far away.... Jer. 30:10

The ships...bring your children from far away, their silver and gold with them for the Name of the Lord your God, and for the Holy One of Israel. Is. 60:9

Your sons shall come from far away, and your daughters shall be carried on their nurses' arms. Is. 60:4

I will signal for them and gather them in, for I have redeemed them, and **they shall be as numerous as they were before**. ...in far countries they shall remember Me, and they shall rear their children and return. Zech. 10:8-9 (They are as many now as before WWII)

Thus says the Lord God: I will soon lift up My hand to the nations and raise My signal to the peoples; and they shall bring your sons in their bosom, and your daughters shall be carried on their shoulders. Is. 49:22

Thus says the Lord God: When I gather the house of Israel from the peoples among whom they are scattered, and manifest My holiness in them in the sight of the nations, then they shall settle on their own soil.... And they shall know that I am the Lord their God. Ezek. 28:25-26

As a pleasing odor I will accept you, when I bring you out from the peoples, and gather you out of the countries where you have been scattered; and I will manifest My holiness among you in the sight of the nations. You shall know that I am the Lord. Ezek. 20:41-42

Safety and Security

In Mount Zion and in Jerusalem there shall be those who escape, as the Lord has said, and among the survivors shall be those whom the Lord calls. Joel 2:23

I will bring them back to this place and I will settle them in safety. Jer. 32: 37

They shall settle on their own soil that I gave to My servant Jacob. They shall live in safety in it, Ezek. 28:25-26

Jacob shall return and have quiet and ease, and no one shall make him afraid. Jer. 30:10

Violence shall no more be heard in your land, devastation or destruction within your borders. Is. 60:18

I will remove the northern army far from you, and drive it into a parched and desolate land, its front into the eastern sea, and its rear into the western sea. Joel 2:20

Jerusalem shall abide in security. Zech. 14:12

Celebrate your festivals, O Judah, fulfill your vows, for never again shall the wicked invade you; they are utterly cut off. Nahum 1:15

Jerusalem shall be inhabited like villages **without walls**, because of the multitude of people and animals in it. For I will be a **wall of fire** all around it, says the Lord, and I will be the **glory** within it. Zech. 2:4

God's Blessing

For I have hidden My face from this city because of all their wickedness. I am going to bring it recovery and healing; I will heal them and reveal to them abundance of prosperity and security. I will restore the fortunes of Judah and the fortunes of Israel, and rebuild them as they were at first. I will cleanse them from all the guilt of their sin ... and rebellion against Me. And this city shall be to Me a name of joy, a praise and a glory before all the nations of the earth who shall hear of all the good that I do for them; they shall fear and tremble because of all the good and all the prosperity I provide for it.... There shall once more be heard the voice of mirth and the voice of gladness, the voice of the bridegroom and the voice of the bride, the voices of those who sing as they bring thank offering to the house of the Lord. Jer. 33:5-11

They [Israel] shall be My people, and I will be their God. I will give them one heart and one way, that they may fear Me for **all time**, for their own good and the good of their children after them. I will make an everlasting covenant with them, never to draw back from doing **good** to them. I will put the fear of Me in their hearts, so that they may not turn from Me. I will **rejoice** {Rejoice!!} in doing good to them, and I will plant them in this land in faithfulness, with **all My heart and all My soul**. Jer. 32: 38-41

Like the days of a tree shall the days of My people be, and My chosen shall long enjoy the work of their hands. They shall not labor in vain, or bear children for calamity; for they shall be offspring blessed by the Lord. Is. 65:22-23

But you, O mountains of Israel, ...I will multiply your population.... They shall increase and be fruitful; and I will cause you to be inhabited as in your former times, ***and will do more good to you than ever before***. Then you shall know that I am the Lord. Ezek. 36:8,10-11

The World Will Notice and Know Why

And they will say, "This land that was desolate has become like the Garden of Eden; and the waste and desolate and ruined towns are now inhabited and fortified." Then the nations that are left all around you shall know that I, the Lord, have rebuilt the ruined places, and replanted that which was desolate; I, the Lord, have spoken, and I will do it. Ezek. 36:35-36

And the nations shall know that the house of Israel went into captivity for their iniquity, because they dealt treacherously with Me. So I hid My face from them and gave them into the hand of their adversaries, and they all fell by the sword. I dealt with them according to their uncleanness and their transgressions, and hid My face from them.... When I have brought them back from the peoples and gathered them from their enemies' lands, and through them have displayed My Holiness in the sight of many nations. Then they shall know that I am the Lord their God because I sent them into exile among the nations, and then gathered them into their own land. I will leave none of them behind; and I will never again hide My face from them, when I pour out My Spirit upon the house of Israel, says the Lord God.
Ezek. 39:21-29

No More Mockery or Being Despised

I am speaking in My jealous wrath because you [Israel] have suffered the insults of the nations; therefore...the nations that are all around you shall themselves suffer insults.
Ezek. 36:7

I will no more make you a mockery among the nations. Joel 2:19

No longer will I let you hear the insults of the nations, no longer shall you bear the disgrace of the peoples..., says the Lord God. Ezek. 36:15

The descendants of those who oppressed you shall come bending low to you, and all who despised you shall bow down at your feet; they shall call you the City of the Lord, the Zion of the Holy One of Israel. Whereas you have been forsaken and hated...I will make you majestic forever, a joy from age to age.... And you shall know that I the Lord, am your Savior and your Redeemer, the Mighty One of Jacob. Is. 60:14-15,16

Thus says the Lord, the Redeemer of Israel and His Holy One, to one deeply despised, abhorred by the nations, the slave of rulers, "Kings shall see and stand up, princes, and they shall prostrate themselves, because of the Lord, who is faithful, the Holy One of Israel, who has chosen you." Is. 49:7

Kings shall be your foster fathers, and their queens your nursing mothers. With their faces to the ground they shall bow down to you, and lick the dust of your feet. Then you will know that I am the Lord. Is. 49:23

No Sacrificing; Won't Miss the Ark

For the Israelites shall remain many days without king or prince, **without sacrifice** or pillar [KJV: image], without ephod [high priest's garment that holds the breastplate] or teraphim [household idols] afterward the Israelites shall return and seek the Lord their God, and David their king, **they shall come in awe to the Lord** and to His goodness **in the latter days**.
Hosea 3:4-5 NIV

And says Adonai, in those days, when your numbers have increased in the land, people will **no longer talk about the ark** for the covenant of Adonai—**they won't think about it**, they **won't miss it** [!], and they **won't make another one [!!]**. When that time comes, they will call Jerusalem the throne of Adonai, all nations will be gathered there to the name of Adonai, to Jerusalem. No longer will they live according to their stubbornly evil hearts. In those days, the house of **Judah will live together with** the house of **Israel**.

Jer. 3:16-18 NIV

Will Mourn the One They Pierced

And I will pour out a spirit of compassion and supplication on the house of David and the inhabitants of Jerusalem, so that, when they look on the One whom they have pierced, they shall mourn for Him, as one mourns for an only child, and weep bitterly over Him, as one weeps over a firstborn. On that day the mourning in Jerusalem will be…great.

Zech. 12:10-11

I will make it like the mourning for an only son, and the end of it like a bitter day.

Amos 8:10

O My poor people put on sackcloth, and roll in ashes; make mourning as for an only child, most bitter lamentation. Jer. 6:26

Last Battle Against Israel

I am going to make Jerusalem a cup that sends all the surrounding peoples reeling…. On that day, when all the nations of the earth are gathered against her, I will make Jerusalem an immovable rock…. All who try to move it will injure [NRSV: grievously hurt] themselves. On that day I will strike every horse with panic and its rider with madness…. On that day the Lord will shield those who live in Jerusalem, so that the feeblest among them will be like David, …like the Angel of the Lord going before them. On that day I will set out to destroy all the nations that attack Jerusalem. Zech. 12:2-4,8-9 NIV

The sovereign Lord says: I am against you, O Gog, …of the land of Magog, …I will turn you around, put hooks in your jaws, and bring you out with your whole army…. Persia, Cush [NRSV: Ethiopia], and Put will be with them…, Gomer…and Beth Togarmah from the far north with all its troops—the many nations with you (NIV). …In the latter years you shall go against a land restored from war…where people were gathered from many nations on the mountains of Israel, which had long lain waste. …And now all of them live in safety. …who are acquiring cattle and goods, who live at the center of the earth (NRSV).

Ezek. 38:1-8,12 NIV then NRSV

You and all your troops and the many nations with you will go up, advancing like a storm; you will be like a cloud covering the land. …Thoughts will come into your mind, and you will devise an evil scheme (NIV). You will say, "I will go up against the land of unwalled villages; I will fall upon the quiet people who live in safety, all of them living without walls…. .

Ezek. 38:9-11 NIV then NRSV

On that day … you will arouse yourself and come from your place out of the remotest parts of the north, you and many peoples with you, all of them riding on horses, a great horde, a mighty army; …. In the latter days I will bring you against My land, so that the nations may know Me…. Ezek. 38: 14-16

Last Battle Against Israel (cont.)

Blow the trumpet in Zion...a great and powerful army comes; like there has never been..., nor will be again.... Before them peoples are in anguish,...they do not swerve from their paths...; they burst through the weapons and are not halted. They leap upon the city, they run upon the walls; ...they climb up into houses.... Joel 2:1,2,6-9

On that day, when Gog comes against the land of Israel, says the Lord God, My wrath shall be aroused. ...There will be a great shaking in the land of Israel; ...and all human beings that are on the face of the earth shall quake at My presence.... I will summon the sword against Gog...; the swords of all will be against their comrades. With pestilence and bloodshed I will enter into judgment with him; and I will pour down torrential rains and hailstones, fire and sulfur, upon him and his troops and the many peoples that are with him. ...Then they shall know that I am the Lord. Ezek. 38:18-23

Prophesy against Gog.... I will strike your bow from your left hand, and will make your arrows drop out of your right hand. On the mountains of Israel you will fall, you and all your troops and the nations with you.... You will fall in the open field; for I have spoken, declares the sovereign Lord. ...Then those who live in the towns of Israel will go out and use the weapons for fuel and burn them up...for seven years. Ezek. 39:1-9 NIV

On that day I will give to Gog a burial place in Israel.... It will block the way of travelers.... For seven months the house of Israel will be burying them....Ezek. 39:11-12 NIV

(In Revelation 20 the battle with Gog is after the millennium, is much fiercer, and is against the whole world. So the two might be different battles altogether.)

Earthquake

On that day His feet shall stand on the Mount of Olives, which lies before Jerusalem on the east; and the Mount of Olives shall be split in two from east to west by a very wide valley; so that one half of the Mount shall withdraw northward, and the other half southward. And you shall flee by the valley of the Lord's mountain, for the valley between the mountains shall reach to Azal. Zech. 14:4-5

What God will do to Israel's Enemies

Truly, one who touches you touches the apple of My eye. See now, I am going to raise My hand against them, and they shall become plunder for their own slaves. Zech. 2:8-9

I will bless those who bless you, and the one who curses you I will curse. Gen. 12:3

Thus says the Lord God: I am speaking in My hot jealousy against the rest of the nations...who with wholehearted joy and utter contempt, took My land as their possession... to plunder it.... I am speaking in My jealous wrath. Ezek. 36:5-6

I, the Lord, have heard all the abusive speech that you uttered against the mountains of Israel.... Thus says the Lord God:... As you rejoiced over...the house of Israel, because it was desolate, so I will deal with you; you shall be desolate. Ezek. 35:12,14,15

Babylon destroyed Jerusalem and took the Jews into captivity in 587 BC.

The word of the Lord.... Declare among the nations and proclaim, set up a banner and proclaim, do not conceal it, say: Babylon is taken...for out of the north a nation has come up against her {Persia came.}; it shall make her land a desolation, and no one shall live in it, both human beings and animals shall flee away.... Her bulwarks have fallen, her walls are thrown down, for this is the vengeance of the Lord...do to her as she has done. Jer. 50:1-4

I will make an end of all the nations among which I scattered you [!], but of you I will not make an end. Jer. 30:11

My people [Israel] have been lost sheep; their shepherds have led them astray.... All who found them have devoured them...and said we are not guilty because they [Israel] have sinned against the Lord. Jer. 50:6-7

They [Israel] shall live in safety, when I execute judgments upon all their neighbors who have treated them with contempt. And they shall know that I am the Lord their God. Ezek. 28:26

Because you cherished an ancient enmity, and gave over the people of Israel to the power of the sword at the time of their calamity, at the time of their final punishment; therefore, as I live, says the Lord God, I will prepare you for blood, and blood shall pursue you.... I will make you a perpetual desolation, and your cities shall never be inhabited. Then you shall know that I am the Lord. Ezek. 35:5-6,9

And the house of Israel will possess the nations as male and female slaves in the Lord's land; they will take captive those who were their captors, and rule over those who oppressed them. Is. 14:2

For the nation and kingdom that will not serve you shall perish; those nations shall be utterly laid waste. Is. 60:12

On that day I will set out to destroy all the nations that attack [NRSV: come against] Jerusalem. Zech. 12:9 NIV

Therefore all who devour you shall be devoured, and all your foes, every one of them, shall go into captivity; those who plunder you shall be plundered, and all who prey on you I will make a prey. Jer. 30:16

Yes, all who are incensed against you shall be ashamed and disgraced; those who strive against you shall be as nothing and shall perish.... Those who war against you shall be as nothing at all. Is. 41:11-12

This shall be the plague with which the Lord will strike all the peoples that wage war against Jerusalem; their flesh shall rot while they are still on their feet; their eyes shall rot in their sockets, and their tongues shall rot in their mouths. On that day a great panic from the Lord shall fall on them, so that each will seize the hand of a neighbor, and the hand of one will be raised against the hand of the other. Zech. 14:12-13

Wealth

At Jerusalem...the wealth of all the surrounding nations shall be collected—gold, silver, and garments in great abundance. Zech. 14:14

Rejoice with Jerusalem, and be glad for her, all you who love her; ...For thus says the Lord: I will extend prosperity to her like a river, and the wealth of the nations like an overflowing stream. Is. 66:10,12

Nations shall bring you their wealth. Is. 60:11

You shall enjoy the wealth of the nations, and in their riches you shall glory. Because [your] shame was double, and dishonor was proclaimed as [your] lot, therefore [you] shall possess a double portion; everlasting joy shall be [yours]. Is. 61:6-7

Then you shall see and be radiant; your heart shall thrill and rejoice, because the abundance of the sea shall be brought to you, the wealth of the nations shall come to you.
Is. 60:5

Nations Shall Come

Ten men **from every language of the nations** shall grasp the sleeve of an **Israelite** saying, "Let us go with you, for we have heard that **God is with you**. Zech. 8:23.

Peoples shall yet come, the inhabitants of many cities; the inhabitants of one city shall go to another, saying, "Come, let us go to entreat the favor of the Lord, and to seek the Lord of hosts; I myself am going." Many peoples and strong nations shall come to seek the Lord of hosts in **Jerusalem**, and to entreat the favor of the Lord. Zech. 8:21-22

The time is coming when Jacob will take root; Israel will bud and flower, and **fill the whole world with a harvest**. Is. 27:6 NIV

In the days to come the mountain of the Lord's house shall be established as the highest of the mountains, and shall be raised above the hills; all the nations shall stream to it. Many people shall come and say, "Come, let us go up to the mountain of the Lord, to the house of the God of Jacob; that He may teach us His ways and that we may walk in His paths. For out of **Zion** shall go forth instruction and the Word of the Lord from **Jerusalem**.
Is. 2:1-4 and Micah 4:1-4

This is what the Lord says, "I will return to Zion and dwell in Jerusalem. Then Jerusalem will be called the City of Truth, and the mountain of the Lord Almighty will be called the Holy Mountain." Zech. 8:3

On that day there will be five cities in the land of Egypt that speak the language of Canaan and swear allegiance to the Lord of hosts. One of these will be called the City of the Sun.... The Lord will make Himself known to the Egyptians; and the Egyptians will know the Lord on that day, and will worship...and He will listen to their supplications and heal them. On that day there will be a highway from Egypt to Assyria, and the Assyrian will come into Egypt, and the Egyptian into Assyria, and **the Egyptians** will worship with the **Assyrians. On that day Israel will be the third with Egypt and Assyria, a blessing in the midst of the earth**, whom the Lord of hosts has blessed. Is. 19:21-24 (Wow!! Let's pray that this soon comes to pass!)

{(But before it happens the Nile has to dry up. I have no idea why!) The waters of the Nile will be dried up...its canals will become foul...reeds and rushes will rot away.... ...and all that is sown by the Nile will dry up, be driven away, and be no more. Those who fish will mourn.... The workers in flax will be in despair, and the carders and those at the loom will grow pale. Its weavers will be dismayed, and all who work for wages will be grieved.... On that day the Egyptians will...tremble with fear before the hand that the Lord of hosts raises against them. And the land of Judah will become a terror to the Egyptians; everyone to whom it is mentioned will fear because of the plan that the Lord of hosts is planning against them (Is. 19:5-10,16-17). All the depths of the Nile will dry up (Zech. 10:11 NIV).}

Sing and rejoice, O daughter Zion! For lo, I will come and dwell in your midst, says the Lord. Many nations shall join themselves to the Lord on that day, and shall be My people and I will dwell in your midst. Zech. 2:10

Aliens will join them and attach themselves to the house of Jacob. Is. 14:1

Then all who survive of the nations that come against Jerusalem shall go up year after year to worship the King, the Lord of hosts, and to keep the festival of booths. If any families of the earth do not go up..., there will be no rain upon them. And if the family (sic.) of Egypt do not go up and present themselves, then on them shall come the plague that the Lord inflicts on the nations that do not go up to keep the festival of the booths.

Zech. 14:16-19

Beautiful Blessings Prophesied for Israel

On that day there shall be inscribed on the bells of the horses, "Holy to the Lord." ...And every cooking pot in Jerusalem and Judah shall be sacred to the Lord.... And there shall no longer be traders in the house of the Lord of hosts on that day. Zech. 14:20-21

You shall eat in plenty and be satisfied, and praise the Name of the Lord your God, who has dealt wondrously with you. And My people shall never again be put to shame. You shall know that I am in the midst of Israel, and that I, the Lord, am your God and there is no other. Joel 2:26-27

The wilderness and the dry land shall be glad, the desert shall rejoice and blossom [as a rose (KJV)]; like the crocus it shall blossom abundantly, and rejoice with joy and singing.... They shall see the Glory of the Lord, the Majesty of our God.... For waters shall break forth in the wilderness and streams in the desert. Is. 35:1-2,6

I will open rivers on the bare heights, and fountains in the midst of the valleys; I will make the wilderness a pool of water, and the dry land springs of water. I will put in the wilderness the cedar, the acacia, the myrtle, and the olive; I will set in the desert the cypress, the plane and the pine together, so that all may see and know, all may consider and understand, that the hand of the Lord has done this, the holy One of Israel has created it.

Is. 41:18-20

On that day living waters shall flow out from Jerusalem, half of them to the eastern sea and half of them to the western sea; it shall continue in summer as in winter.... The whole land shall be turned into a plain.... But Jerusalem shall remain aloft.... And it shall be inhabited, for never again shall it be doomed to destruction. Zech. 14:5-11

Sing, O heavens, for the Lord has done it; shout, O depths of the earth; break forth into singing, O mountains, O forest, and every tree in it! For the Lord has redeemed Jacob, and will be glorified in Israel. Is. 44:23

(There are many more prophecies about Israel you can list here.)
(I know. I said I wouldn't bother you again, but I can't help myself. ; 0)

PRAYER FOR ISRAEL

Dec. 22, '05 (In Jerusalem in the Old City)

As I knelt with my face to the floor and prayed, Jesus turned my thoughts to all the street markets vendors who hound us as we try to walk around in Jerusalem, and to the condition of Jerusalem and how it makes me feel sad. It is not a city of peace, or of praise, or of worship in awe to God. It is a city of busy-ness, of merchants yelling and pressuring, of crowdedness and chaos.

I began to pray for the vendors and the crowds of people who live here that they would find Jesus. Then I remembered that this is the city Jesus wept over:

"O Jerusalem, Jerusalem the city that kills the prophets and stones those who are sent to it? How often have I desired to gather your children together as a hen gathers her brood under her wings and you were not willing. See, your house is left to you desolate. For I tell you, you will not see me again until you say, 'Blessed is the One who comes in the Name of the Lord.'" Matt. 23:37-39

Jesus cried over this city and it makes me feel like crying, too.

O Jesus, You must still be weeping and weeping. This city has been judged and completely destroyed. Twice. The first time was just as Jeremiah prophesied it would be by Babylon; the second time by Rome just as You prophesied, Jesus. The temple has been contaminated five or six times with the "abomination of desolation" as Daniel prophesied! By the Babylonians, the Greeks, the Romans, the Persians, the Crusaders (who conquered, killed, and burned Jewish women and children in synagogues), and the Muslims. Surely that is enough times, Jesus. Please, let it be enough.

It is being "trampled by the Gentiles" as You prophesied, Jesus, "until the times of the Gentiles are fulfilled" (Lk. 21:24). O Jesus, let the times of the Gentiles be fulfilled. Bring it to fulfillment. Surely, Jesus, it has been long enough to have the "desolating sacrifice" in the Holy of Holies. Surely 1,930 plus years is enough time! Let it be enough, Jesus. We don't have to wait anymore, do we? Please, don't let Your city suffer any longer, Jesus. Please release your city from its chains and its darkness. Please set Jerusalem free from evil. Set Israel free. Set the world free. Set all your people free. Set the Jews and the Gentiles free.

Do as You promised through Jeremiah, Lord. Bring Your Word to pass. You fulfilled Your Words of doom. They have come to pass. Five or more times Jerusalem has been conquered. At least thrice she has been burned to the ground. At least four times there has been the "abomination" in the temple by at least four different kingdoms. Now bring to pass Your promises of glory and blessing for Jerusalem.

*I will give them one heart and one way, that they may fear Me for **all time**, ... I will make an everlasting covenant with them, never to draw back from doing good to them.... I will **rejoice** {Rejoice!!} in doing good to them, and I will plant them in this land in faithfulness, with **all My heart and all My soul**.* Jer. 32: 37-41

O Jesus, You **want** to do this with all Your heart and all Your soul. All Your HUGE, MAGNIFICENT, LOVING HEART. Your big eternal, loving, merciful heart!!!!

O Jesus, Father, Holy Spirit, bring to pass this desire of Your heart and soul! Bring it to pass for Jerusalem, for Israel, for all Your people, the Jews, for all the descendants and seed of Abraham—even all the descendants through Ishmael! Do it for all the inhabitants of Jerusalem and Israel—for all the nations of the earth represented in all the people dwelling here in Israel!

O Jesus, let not Your heart be broken anymore. Let not Your soul be grieved any longer! Bring it to pass that You may rejoice in doing good for Jerusalem and Your people. Let all the families of the earth be blessed through what You do for Jerusalem and her people!

Let all the people here in Jerusalem, Jews—Orthodox, Hassadim, Reform, and non worshipers; and Muslims—radical and moderate, let them all praise You, Jesus. Let them come together in unity, in one heart and one soul to praise You and to say, "Blessed is He who comes in the Name of the Lord!!!" Let them welcome You with open arms and melted hearts—ready to receive You as Lord and Messiah.

Remove from them the spirit of legalism and the spirit of false religion, the spirit of deceit and blindness and of deafness. May all those spirits be removed from Jerusalem and Israel and be bound in eternal chains and cast into the everlasting Lake of Fire to burn forever. Amen Hallelujah! By the power and authority and Name of Jesus Christ, crucified and resurrected and ascended!

In the Name of Jesus, by the Power of the Blood of Jesus of Nazareth, the Messiah, the Son of the Most High, LIVING GOD, I rebuke you spirit of hatred. Be removed from Jerusalem. Be thou removed! BE GONE. Be cast into the Lake of Fire. I speak to you spirit of radical Islam. Be GONE. Be removed and cast into the Lake of Fire. Be removed from all of Israel. Be removed from the face of the earth in Jesus' Holy Name; by the Power and authority of Jesus' Name.

Be gone spirit of Jihad. Be gone spirit of terrorism. Be gone. Be cast into the Lake of Fire. Spirit of anti-Christ, be removed and cast into the Lake of Fire. Spirits against Christ—every spirit against the True Messiah, be removed from Jerusalem and from Israel and cast into the Lake of Fire FOREVER, never to come out again against Jesus and His people!! Never again to desecrate Jesus' Holy City! Never again to desecrate Jesus' people. Be bound up in chains! Come out from your strongholds. Strongholds, be torn down! Be crumbled to the ground. Be crushed into powder. Spirits against Jesus, come out of your strongholds and be bound in chains, and be removed and cast into the Lake of Fire to be burned forever and ever by the Power and Authority of the Blood of Jesus the Messiah and the Name of JESUS CHRIST, CRUCIFIED AND RISEN REDEEMER!!!

Let it be so! Let it come to pass, Jesus, Holy Spirit, Father. Bring it to pass. Let Your will be done. BRING YOUR WILL TO PASS!!!

In all its towns there shall again be pasture for shepherds resting their flocks...flocks shall again pass under the hand of the One who counts them (Jer. 33:12-13). O Lord Jesus, bring Your Word to pass. Bless this city. Let there be pasture for Your sheep. Let there be rest for Your sheep. Let there be pastors for them who love them. NO, rather let **You** be their shepherd. Amen, Hallelujah!! BRING YOUR PROMISES TO PASS! You promised, Father, JESUS, Holy Spirit. You PROMISED! Bring all Your promises to pass!! Let is be so!!

I will give them one heart and one way, that they may fear Me for all time, for their own good and the good of their children after them (Jer. 32:39). Yes, let all the people of Jerusalem unite in one heart and one soul and one way to say, "Blessed is the One who comes in the Name of the Lord Jesus!" One way, Jesus, YOUR WAY—THE WAY OF THE CROSS!!! Come, Lord Jesus, come quickly Your people, Your Bride is waiting for You!

Jan. 31, '06

As regarding election they are beloved. For the gifts and the calling of God are irrevocable (Rom. 11:28-29). The article I'm reading says this verse is clearly showing that the Jewish culture is God's gifts and God's call! That Messianic Jews need to live their Jewish culture.

It makes me ponder the tug of my heart toward my Plain clothes roots and to my friends who are still living the Plain life. There is value in that life. There is a peace and a stability the rest of the world lacks. Yet that way of life is lacking something.

It is lacking what the Biblical Jewish culture is not lacking! Meaning! Deep meaning in every aspect of it! The Plain culture has mostly abstaining and cloistering. The Orthodox Jewish culture has that, too, but it has so much more. Yet both are still lacking something. The ***Messianic*** Jewish culture has all that the other two have, PLUS ABUNDANT LIFE! It has it all!

Dear Jesus, the Jewish culture is so beautiful because You designed and created it. It is all about You. It points to You. And You are the One who is fulfilling it. You are the One who gives it all its deep meaning. Living it without You makes it worth nothing. But even living it with You, because we are human, we usually end up contaminating it with lifeless legalism, or dominating control-ism, or dull ritualism.

I look forward to the day of Your coming when we will live it together with You in all its fulfillment. Bring that day, Jesus. Let it come to pass. It will be a life full of pure righteousness, perfect peace, and sheer joy in the Holy Spirit. And it will have a depth of meaning that we cannot begin to fathom here on earth.

While we are waiting for that day, I pray that more and more Jewish people will come to know You as the reason and meaning behind all their feasts and traditions. And I pray for the Plain people that they will realize they have something of value that the world needs, even their Christian brothers and sisters. I pray they will come to know You in a deeper way until they have Your burden for the world and begin as whole communities, not just individuals, to carry out Your Great Commission.

(Go ahead and express your heart for Israel here.)

Jesus told them...about their need to pray and not to lose heart. Luke 18:1

"Be alert at all times, praying." Luke 21:36

Prophecies about
Jesus' Second Coming

What surprised me most about this whole book, but about this section in particular, is how many times things are repeated in the Bible. If the Ruler of the Universe says anything, it is very important! We had better listen! If He says it twice we had better sit up, take note, and ponder! If He says it several times—well! Nothing can possibly describe how important it must be! We had better think hard on it every day, all day. Take a look at how many times He repeats things about the Second Coming—even in the Old Testament! I am astounded!

Before the End: Wars, Earthquake, Persecution

"For nation will rise against nation, and kingdom against kingdom, and there will be famines and earthquakes in various places: all this is but the beginning of the birth pangs."
Matt. 24:7-8

"For nation will rise against nation, and kingdom against kingdom; there will be earthquakes in various places; there will be famines. This is but the beginning of the birth pangs." Mk. 13:8

"Nation will rise against nation, and kingdom against kingdom; there will be great earthquakes, and in various places famines and plagues; and there will be dreadful portents and great signs from heaven" Lk. 21:10

The end will come like a flood: War will continue until the end, and desolations have been decreed. Dan. 9:26 NIV

"And you will be hated by all because of My Name." Mk. 13:13
"You will be hated by all because of My Name." Lk. 21:17
"You will be betrayed even by parents and brothers, by relatives and friends."
Lk. 21:16

"Many will fall away, and they will betray one another and hate one another."
Matt. 24:10

"They will put some of you to death." Lk. 21:16b

Those who are wise will instruct many, though for a time they will fall by the sword or be burned or captured or plundered. Dan. 11:33 NIV (Missionaries? Martyrs?)

When they fall victim, they shall receive a little help, and many shall join them insincerely. Dan. 11:34

" And because of the increase of lawlessness, the love of many will grow cold."
Matt. 24:12

Some of the wise shall fall, so that they may be refined, purified, and cleansed, until the time of the end, for there is still an interval until the time appointed. Dan. 11:35

...Until the time of the end. Many shall be running back and forth, and evil shall increase. [NKJV: and knowledge shall increase.] [NIV: Many will go here and there to increase knowledge.] Dan. 12:4

Terrorists

See, I am stirring up the Medes against them, who have no regard for silver and do not delight in gold. Their bows will slaughter the young men; they will have no mercy on the fruit of the womb; their eyes will not pity children. Is. 13:18

In the street the sword...and in the chamber terror, for young...and old. Deut. 32:25

"We have heard news of them, our hands fall helpless; anguish has taken hold of us, pain as of a woman in labor. Do not go out into the field, or walk on the road; for the enemy has a sword, terror is on every side." Jer. 6:24-25

Thus says the Lord: We have heard a cry of panic, of terror, and no peace. ... Can a man bear a child? Why then do I see every man with his hands on his loins like a woman in labor? Why has every face turned pale? Alas! That day is so great there is none like it. It is a time of distress for Jacob; yet he shall be rescued from it. Jer. 30:5-7

"Every heart will melt and all hands will be feeble, every spirit will faint and all knees will turn to water. See, it comes and it will be fulfilled," says the Lord God. Ezek. 21:7

Terror and the pit, and the snare are upon you, O inhabitant of the earth! Whoever flees at the sound of the terror shall fall into the pit; and whoever climbs out of the pit shall be caught in the snare. Is. 24:17-18

There will be a time of distress [NRSV: anguish] such as has not happened from the beginning of nations until then. [NRSV: has never occurred since nations first came into existence.] Dan. 12:1 NIV

There they shall be in great terror, in terror such as has not been. Ps. 53:5

Thus says the Lord God: Remove the turban, take off the crown; things shall not remain as they are.... A ruin, a ruin, a ruin—I will make it! Such has never occurred. Until He comes whose right it is; to Him I will give it. Ezek. 21: 26:27

When the overwhelming scourge passes through you will be beaten down by it. As often as it passes through, it will take you; for morning by morning it will pass through, by day and by night; and it will be sheer terror. Is. 28:18-19

One who trusts will not panic. Is. 28:24

Near the End

"And this Good News of the kingdom will be proclaimed throughout the world, as a testimony to all the nations; and then the end will come." Matt. 24:14

"And the Good News must first be proclaimed to all nations." Mk. 13:10

"Lord, is this the time...?" He replied, ..."You will be my witnesses...to the ends of the earth." Acts 1:6,8

Then I saw another angel flying in midheaven, with an Eternal Gospel to proclaim to those who live on the earth—to every nation and tribe and language and people. He said in a loud voice, "Fear God and give Him glory, for the hour of His judgment has come.
Rev. 14:6

...Until the full number of the Gentiles has come in. Rom. 11:25

...It [Jerusalem] has been given to the Gentiles. They will trample the holy city for 42 months. Rev. 11:2 NIV

And Jerusalem will be trampled on by the Gentiles, until the times of the Gentiles are fulfilled. Lk. 21:24

One of them said..., "How long shall it be until the end....?" ...And I heard him swear by the One who lives forever that...when the shattering of the power of the holy people comes to an end, all these things would be accomplished. Dan. 12:6-7

When you see these things

"Now when these things begin to take place, stand up and raise your heads, because your redemption is drawing near." Lk. 21:28

"So, also when you see these things taking place, you know that the Kingdom of God is near." Lk. 21:31

"So, ...when you see these things taking place, you know that He is near, at the very gates. ...[T]his generation {I assume the one that starts to see these things happen.} will not pass away until all these things have taken place." Mk. 13:29-30, Matt. 24:33-34

No One Knows the Exact Time of the End

But about that day and hour no one knows, neither the angels of heaven, nor the Son, but only the Father. Matt. 24:36, Mk. 13:32

"Lord is this the time...?" He replied, "It is not for you to know the times or periods that the Father has set by His own authority." Acts 1:6-8

Therefore, beloved, while you are waiting for these things, strive to be found by Him at peace, without spot or blemish; and regard the patience of our Lord as salvation. II Pet. 2:14-15

Keep Awake! Be Alert!

But the day of the Lord will come like a thief. II Pet. 2:10

Now concerning the times and the seasons...the day of the Lord will come like a thief in the night. When they say, "There is peace and security," then sudden destruction will come upon them, as labor pains come upon a pregnant woman, and there will be no escape!
I Thess. 5:1-3

"Keep awake therefore, for you do not know on what day your Lord is coming."
Matt. 24:42

"Be ready, for the Son of Man is coming at an unexpected hour." Matt. 24:44

Be on guard so that your hearts are not weighed down with dissipation [dictionary definition: wasteful indulgence in pleasure, amusement; a diversion] and drunkenness and the worries of this life, and that day does not catch you unexpectedly, like a trap. Lk. 21:34

For as the days of Noah were, so will be the coming of the Son of Man. For as in those days before the flood they were eating and drinking, [and] marrying ...and they knew nothing until the flood came and swept them all away, so too will be the coming of the Son of Man.
Matt. 24:37-39 and Lk. 17:26-27

Just as in the days of Lot: they were eating and drinking, buying and selling, planting and building, but on the day that Lot left Sodom, it rained fire and sulfur from heaven and destroyed all of them—it will be like that on the day that the Son of Man is revealed.
Lk. 17:28-30:

"Blessed is that slave whom his Master will find at work when He arrives." Matt.24:46

"But if...he [the slave] begins to beat his fellow-slaves, and eats and drinks with drunkards, the master of that slave will come on a day when he does not expect Him and at an hour that he does not know. He will cut him in pieces and put him with the hypocrites, where there will be weeping and gnashing of teeth." Matt. 24:48-51

Behold, I come quickly; and My reward is with Me, to give every man according as his work shall be. Rev. 22:12 KJV

See, I am coming soon! Blessed is the one who keeps the Words...of this book [the Bible]. Rev. 22:7

Christ is coming a second time...to save those who are eagerly waiting for Him. Heb. 9:28

Prepare to meet your God! Amos 4:12

The Righteous Shall be Protected

Be alert at all times, praying that you may have the strength to escape all these things that will take place, and to stand before the Son of Man. Lk. 21:36

If you do not wake up, I will come like a thief, and you will not know at what hour I will come to you. Rev. 3:3 This can imply that if we are awake, we will have an idea when His coming is near. These next couple verses also imply that we should be able to tell when the time is near.

"You hypocrites! You know how to interpret the earth and sky, but why do you not know how to interpret the present time?" Lk. 12;56

But you, beloved, are not in darkness, for that day to surprise you like a thief; for you are all children of light and children of the day; we are not of the night or of darkness. So then let us not fall asleep as others do, but let us keep awake and be sober; for those who sleep sleep at night, and those who are drunk get drunk at night. But since we belong to the day, let us be sober.... For God has destined us not for wrath but for obtaining salvation through our Lord Jesus Christ, who died for us. I Thess. 5:4-9

Because you have kept my Word of patient endurance, I will keep you from the hour of trial that is coming on the whole world to test the inhabitants of the earth. Rev. 3:10

Seek the Lord, all you humble of the land, who do His commands; seek righteousness, seek humility; perhaps you may be hidden on the day of the Lord's wrath. Zeph. 2:3

Pray that you may not come into the time of trial. Lk. 22:40 Stay awake and pray that you may not come into the time of trial. Mt. 26:41, Mk. 14:38.

You shall be hidden...and shall not fear destruction when it comes. At destruction and famine, you shall laugh. Job 5:21-22

For the righteous are taken away from calamity and they enter into peace, those who walk uprightly will rest on their couches. Is. 57:1

Come, My people, enter your chambers and shut your doors behind you. Hide yourselves for awhile until wrath is past. For the Lord comes out from His place to punish the inhabitants of the earth for their iniquity. Is. 26:20-21

At that time Michael, the great prince, the protector of your people, shall arise. There shall be a time of anguish, such as has never occurred since nations first came into existence. But at that time your people shall be delivered, everyone who is found written in the book. Dan. 12:1

"And yet, when the Son of Man comes, will He find faith on earth?" Lk. 18:8

May the God of peace...sanctify you entirely; and may your spirit and soul and body be kept sound and blameless at the coming of our Lord Jesus Christ. I Thess. 5:23

False Prophets and Deception

"Then if anyone says to you, 'Look! Here is the Messiah!' or 'There he is!'—do not believe it. For false messiahs and false prophets will appear and produce great signs and omens, to lead astray, if possible, even the elect." Matt. 24:23-24

"And if anyone says to you at that time, 'Look! Here is the Messiah!' or 'Look! There he is!'—do not believe it. False messiahs and false prophets will appear and produce signs and omens, to lead astray, if possible, the elect." Mk. 13:21-22

"So, if they say to you, 'Look! He is in the wilderness,' do not go out. If they say, "Look! He is in the inner rooms,' do not believe it. For as the lightning comes from the east and flashes as far as the west, so will be the coming of the Son of Man." Matt. 24:26

All Shall See

"The days are coming when you will long to see one of the days of the Son of Man, and you will not see it. They will say to you, 'Look there!' or "Look here!' Do not go, do not set off in pursuit. For as the lightning flashes and lights up the sky...so will the Son of Man be in His day." Lk. 17:23-24

"Then the sign of the Son of Man will appear in heaven, and then all the tribes of the earth will mourn, they will see 'the Son of Man coming on the clouds of heaven' with Power and great Glory." Matt. 24:30

Then the Glory of the Lord shall be revealed, and all people shall see it together, for the mouth of the Lord has spoken. Is. 40:5

"When the Son of man comes in His Glory, and all the angels with Him, then He will sit on the throne of His Glory. All the nations will be gathered before Him." Matt. 25:31

All the human beings that are on the face of the earth shall quake at My presence.
Ezek. 38:20

"For it will come upon all who live on the face of the whole earth." Lk. 21:35

...the hour of trial that is coming on the whole world to test the inhabitants of the earth. Rev. 3:10

Let us know, let us press on to **know** the Lord. His appearing is as sure as the dawn. He will come to us like showers; like the spring rains that water the earth. Hos. 6:3

The Rapture (Even in the Old Testament!)

I saw One like a human being [note: Son of Man] coming with the clouds of heaven.
Dan. 7:13

"Then the sign of the Son of Man will appear in heaven, ...they will see 'the Son of Man coming on the clouds of heaven' with Power and great Glory. And He will send out His angels with a loud trumpet call, and they will gather His elect from the four winds, from one end of heaven to the other." Matt. 24:30-32

"Then they will see 'the Son of Man coming in clouds' with great Power and Glory. Then He will send out the angels, and gather His elect from the four winds, from the ends of the earth to the ends of heaven." Mk. 13:26-27

I am coming to gather all nations and tongues and they shall come and shall see My Glory. Is. 66:18

...when the Lord Jesus is revealed from heaven with His mighty angels in flaming fire,...[in] the Glory of His might, when He comes to be glorified by His saints and to be marveled at on that day.... II Thess. 1:6-10

"Hereafter you will see the Son of Man sitting at the right hand of the Power, and coming on the clouds of heaven." Matt. 26:64 NKJV

"...when He comes in the Glory of His Father with the holy angels." Mk. 8:38

Then I looked, and there was a white cloud, and seated on the cloud was One like the Son of Man, with a golden crown on His head, and a sharp sickle in His hand! Another angel came out of the temple, calling with a loud voice to the One who sat on the cloud, "Use Your sickle and reap, for the hour to reap has come, because the harvest of the earth is fully ripe." So the One who sat on the cloud swung His sickle over the earth, and the earth was reaped. Rev. 14:14-16

Rapture (Even in the Old Testament!) (cont.)

"Then two will be in the field; one will be taken and one will be left. Two women will be grinding meal together; one will be taken and one will be left." Matt. 24: 40

I tell you, on that night there will be two in one bed; one will be taken and the other left. There will be two women grinding meal together; one will be taken and the other left. Lk. 17:34-35

When I wanted to gather them, says the Lord, there are (sic) no grapes on the vine.... Grief is upon Me, My heart is sick. Hark, the cry of My poor people from far and wide, ..."The harvest is past, the summer is ended, and we are not saved." Jer. 8:13,18-19,20

Listen, I will tell you a mystery! We will not all die, but we will all be changed, in a moment, in the twinkling of an eye, at the last trumpet. For the trumpet will sound, and the dead will be raised imperishable, and we will be changed...When this perishable body puts on imperishability, and this mortal body puts on immortality. I Cor. 15:51-54

This we declare to you by the Word of the Lord.... The Lord Himself, with a cry of command, with the archangel's call and with the sound of God's trumpet, will descend from heaven, and the dead in Christ will rise first. Then we who are alive, who are left, will be caught up in the clouds together with them to meet the Lord in the air; and so we will be with the Lord forever. Therefore encourage one another with these words. I Thess. 4:15,16-18

God has gone up with a shout, the Lord with the sound of a trumpet. Ps. 47:5
On the third day He will raise us up that we may live before Him. Hos. 6:2
When Christ who is our life appears, then you also will appear with Him in Glory. Col. 3:4 NKJV
All...you who live on the earth,...when a trumpet is blown, listen! Is. 18:3
On that day a great trumpet will be blown, and those who were lost...will come and worship the Lord on the holy mountain in Jerusalem. Is. 27:13 (The new Jerusalem?!)

The devout are taken away while no one understands. For the righteous are taken away from calamity. Is. 57:1

Many of those who sleep in the dust of the earth shall awake, some to everlasting life, and some to shame and everlasting contempt. Those who are wise shall shine like the brightness of the sky, and those who lead many to righteousness, like the stars forever and ever. Dan.12:2-3

They will sparkle in His land like jewels in a crown. How attractive and beautiful they will be! Zech. 9:16-17 NIV

He set forth in Christ...a plan for the fullness of time to gather up all things in Him, things in heaven and things on earth...for the praise of His Glory. Eph. 1:9-10,12

Then they heard a loud voice from heaven saying to them, "Come up here!" And they went up to heaven in a cloud while their enemies watched them. At that moment there was a great earthquake, and a tenth of the city fell; seven thousand people were killed in the earthquake, and the rest were terrified and gave glory to the God of heaven. Rev. 11:12-13

Sun, Moon and Stars

There will be signs in the sun, the moon, and the stars, and on the earth distress among nations confused by the roaring of the sea and the waves. People will faint from fear and foreboding of what is coming upon the world, for the powers of the heavens will be shaken. Lk. 21:25-26

The fourth angel blew his trumpet, and a third of the sun was struck, and a third of the moon, and a third of the stars, so that a third of their light was darkened; a third of the day was kept from shining, and likewise the night.... And I heard an eagle crying... "Woe, woe, woe to the inhabitants of the earth." Rev. 8:12-13

Immediately after the suffering of those days the sun will be darkened, and the moon will not give its light; the stars will fall from heaven, and the powers of heaven will be shaken. Matt. 24:29

But in those days, after that suffering,
the sun will be darkened,
and the moon will not give its light,
and the stars will be falling from heaven,
and the powers in the heavens will be shaken. Mk. 13:24-25

The sun and the moon are darkened, and the stars withdraw their shining. Joel 3:15

For the stars of the heavens and their constellations will not give their light; the sun will be dark at its rising, and the moon will not shed its light. Is. 13:10

Because of this the earth shall mourn, and the heavens above grow black. Jer. 4:23

The earthquakes before them, the heavens tremble. The sun and the moon are darkened, and the stars withdraw their shining. Joel 2:10

For lo, the One who...makes the morning darkness...—the Lord, the God of Hosts, is His Name! Amos 4:13

Look to the land—only darkness and distress; and the light grows dark with clouds. Is. 5:30

They meet with darkness in the daytime and grope at noonday as in the night. Job 5:14

I clothe the heavens with blackness, and make sackcloth their covering. Is. 50:3

When I blot you out, I will cover the heavens, and make their stars dark; I will cover the sun with a cloud, and the moon shall not give its light. All the shining lights of the heavens I will darken above you, and put darkness on your land, says the Lord God. Ezek. 32:7-8

On that day, says the Lord God, I will make the sun go down at noon, and darken the earth in broad daylight. I will turn your feasts into mourning, and all your songs into lamentation; I will bring sackcloth on all loins, and baldness on every head; I will make it like the mourning for an only son, and the end of it like a bitter day. Amos 8:10

Therefore it shall be night to you, without vision and darkness to you, without revelation. The sun shall go down upon the prophets, and the day shall be black over them. Micah 3:5-8

While you look for light, He turns it into gloom and makes it deep darkness. Is. 13:16

Sun, Moon and Stars (Cont.)

That day will be a day of wrath, a day of distress and anguish, a day of ruin and devastation, a day of darkness and gloom, a day of clouds and thick darkness. Zeph.1:15

For darkness shall cover the earth, and thick darkness the peoples; Is. 60:2

And the sun and the air were darkened with the smoke from the shaft. Rev. 9:2

Let all the inhabitants of the land tremble for the day of the Lord is coming, it is near—a day of darkness and gloom, a day of clouds and thick darkness! Like blackness spread upon the mountains.... I will show portents in the heavens and on the earth, blood and fire and columns of smoke. The sun shall be turned to darkness, and the moon to blood, before the great and terrible day of the Lord comes. Then everyone who calls on the Name of the Lord shall be saved. Joel 2:1-2,30-31

The fifth angel poured his bowl on the throne of the beast, and its kingdom was plunged into darkness; people gnawed their tongues in agony, and cursed the God of heaven. Rev. 16:10

I looked, and there came a great earthquake; the sun became black as sackcloth, the full moon became like blood, and the stars of the sky fell to the earth.... The sky vanished like a scroll rolling itself up. Rev. 6:12-14

And the moon will be abashed and the sun ashamed, for the Lord of hosts will reign... He will manifest His Glory. Is. 24:23

Removal of All Evil

"The Son of Man will send His angels, and they will collect out of His kingdom all causes of sin and all evildoers, and they will throw them into the furnace of fire, where there will be weeping and gnashing of teeth. Then the righteous will shine like the sun in the kingdom of their Father." Matt. 13:41-43

"The weeds are the children of the evil one.... Just as the weeds are collected and burned up with fire, so will it be at the end of the age." Matt. 13:38-40

Rebels and sinners...and those who forsake the Lord shall be consumed. Is. 1:28

The eyes of the Lord are upon the sinful kingdom; and I will destroy it from the face of the earth. Amos 9:8

I will purge out the rebels among you, and those who transgress against Me. Ezek. 20:38

The locusts were like horses equipped for battle. ...[T]hey had scales like iron..., and the noise of their wings was like the noise of many chariots with horses rushing into battle. ...[I]n their tails is their power to harm people for five months. Rev. 9:7,9-10

They [the locusts] were told...to damage...only those people who do not have the seal of God on their foreheads. They were allowed to torture them for five months, but not to kill them.... And...people will...long to die, but death will flee from them. Rev. 9:4-5

The number of the troops of calvary was two hundred million.... Fire and sulphur came out of their mouths. By these three plagues a third of humankind was killed, by the fire and smoke and sulfur.... For the power of the horses is in their mouths and in their tails.... The rest of humankind, who were not killed by these plagues, did not repent.... Rev. 9:16-20

See, the day of the Lord comes, cruel, with wrath and fierce anger, to make the earth a desolation, and to destroy its sinners from it. Is. 13:9

Removal of All Evil (Cont.)

The tyrant shall be no more, and the scoffer shall cease to be; all those alert to do evil shall be cut off. Is. 29:20

May...evildoers nevermore be named! ...Let them never rise to possess the earth. Is. 14:20-21

Put in sickle for the harvest is ripe. Go in, tread, for the wine press is full. The vats overflow, for their wickedness is great. Joel 3:13

So the angel swung his sickle over the earth and gathered the vintage of the earth, and he threw it into the great wine press of the wrath of God. Rev. 14:19

He will tread the wine press of the fury of the wrath of God the Almighty. Rev.19:15

"Who is this so splendidly robed, marching in His great might?" (cont.)

"It is I, announcing vindication, mighty to save." (cont.)

"Why are Your robes red and Your garments like theirs who tread the wine press?" (cont.)

"I have trodden the wine press alone, and from the peoples no one was with Me; I trod them in My anger and trampled them in My wrath; their juice spattered on My garments, and stained all My robes. For the day of vengeance was in My heart, and the year for My redeeming work had come." Is. 63:1-4

...He washes His garments in wine and His robe in the blood of grapes. Gen. 49:11

And the wine press was trodden outside the city, and blood flowed from the wine press. Rev. 14:20

Anti-Christ and the Beast and Deception

And every spirit that does not confess Jesus is not from God. And this is the spirit of the antichrist, of which you have heard that it is coming; and now it is already in the world. I Jn. 4:3

Let no one deceive you in any way; for that day will not come unless the rebellion comes first and the lawless one is revealed, the one destined for destruction. He opposes and exalts himself above every so-called god or object of worship, so that he takes his seat in the temple of God declaring himself to be God.... And you know what is now restraining him, so that he may be revealed when his time comes. For the mystery of lawlessness is already at work, but only until the one who now restrains it is removed. And then the lawless one will be revealed, whom the Lord Jesus will destroy with the breath of His mouth, annihilating him by the manifestation of His coming. The coming of the lawless one is apparent in the working of satan, who uses all power, signs, lying wonders, and every kind of wicked deception for those who are perishing, because they refused to love the truth and so be saved. II Thess. 2:3-10

By his cunning he shall make deceit prosper under his hand and in his own mind he shall be great. Dan. 8:25

He shall pay no respect to any other god, for he shall consider himself greater than all. Dan. 11:37

He shall make sacrifice and offering cease; and in their place shall be an abomination that desolates, until the decreed end is poured out upon the desolator. Dan. 9:27

He shall speak words against the Most High. Dan 9:25

...and a mouth speaking arrogantly...because of the noise of the arrogant words that the horn [beast] was speaking. Dan 7:8,11

Anti-Christ and the Beast and Deception (Cont.)

You who laid the nations low! You said in your heart., "I will raise my throne above the stars of God; ...I will make myself like the Most High." Is. 14:12

The beast...opened its mouth to utter blasphemies against God, blaspheming His Name and His dwelling. Rev. 13:6

It [the beast] performs great signs, even making fire come down from heaven to earth in the sight of all; and by the signs that it is allowed to perform, ...it deceives the inhabitants of the earth.... Rev. 13:13,14

The Dragon, Beast, and Death Destroyed

A great red dragon, with seven heads and ten horns...his tail swept down a third of the stars of heaven and threw them to the earth. Rev. 12:3-4

It grew as high as the host of heaven, It threw down to the earth some of the host and some of the stars, and trampled on them. Dan. 8:10

"The stars will fall from heaven, and the powers of heaven will be shaken." Matt. 24:29

The stars of the sky fell to the earth as the fig tree drops its winter fruit when shaken by a gale. Rev. 6:13

The great dragon was thrown down, that ancient serpent, who is called the devil and satan, the deceiver of the whole world.... Rev. 12:9

[Jesus said] "I watched satan fall from heaven like a flash of lightning." Lk. 10:18

How you are fallen from heaven, O lucifer, son of the morning! How you are cut down to the ground. Is. 14:12 NKJV

These are united in yielding their power and authority to the beast; they will make war on the Lamb, and the Lamb will conquer them, for He is Lord of Lords and King of Kings, and those with Him are called and chosen and faithful. Rev. 17:13-14

Without warning he...shall even rise up against the Prince of Princes. But he [the beast] shall be broken, and not by human hands. Dan. 8:25

He [Jesus] seized the dragon, that ancient serpent, who is the devil and satan, and bound him for a thousand years, and threw him into the pit, and locked and sealed it over him. Rev. 20:1-3

On that day the Lord will punish the host of heaven in heaven, {This is the second heaven, the realm where the demons are.} and on earth the kings of the earth. They will be gathered together like prisoners in a pit; they will be shut up in a prison, and after many days they will be punished. Is. 24:21-22

All the hosts of heaven shall rot away, {Again, this is the second heaven where the demons dwell.} and the skies shall roll up like a scroll. All their hosts shall wither like a leaf withering on a vine or fruit withering on a fig tree. Is. 34:4 {Jesus withered a fig tree! And He told us we can do the same or more! See Matt. 21:18-22}

The Dragon, Beast, and Death Destroyed (Cont.)

You who laid the nations low! You said in your heart..., "I will make myself like the Most High." But you are brought down to Shoel, to the depths of the Pit. Those who see you will stare at you...who made the earth tremble, ...who made the world like a desert, ...who would not let his prisoners go home, ...but you are cast out, ...like loathsome carrion...like a corpse trampled underfoot, ...because you have destroyed...people. Is. 14:12-20

God did not spare the angels when they sinned, but cast them into hell and committed them to chains of deepest darkness to be kept until the judgment. II Pet. 2:4

The angels who did not keep their own position, but left their proper dwelling, He has kept in eternal chains in deepest darkness for the judgment of the great Day. Jude 6

On that day the Lord with His cruel and great and strong sword will punish Leviathan the fleeing serpent, Leviathan the twisting serpent, and He [the Lord] will kill the dragon that is in the sea. Is. 27:1

And I saw a beast rising out of the sea, having ten horns and seven heads ... and on its heads were blasphemous names. Rev. 13;1

You broke the heads of the dragons of the waters. You crushed the heads of Leviathan. You gave him as food for the creatures of the wilderness. Ps. 74:13-14

The great dragon sprawling in the midst of its channels, ...I will put hooks in your jaws, and make the fish of your channels stick to your scales. I will draw you up from your channels, with all the fish of your channels sticking to your scales. I will fling you into the wilderness....you shall fall in the open field, and not be gathered and buried. To the animals of the earth and to the birds of the air I have given you as food. Ezek. 29:3,4,5

And the rest were killed by the sword of the Rider on the horse, the sword that came from His mouth; and all the birds were gorged with their flesh. Rev. 19:21

And then shall that wicked one be revealed, whom the Lord shall consume with the Spirit of His mouth, and shall destroy with the brightness of His coming. II Thess. 2:8

Then I saw the beast and the kings of the earth with their armies gathered to make war against the Rider on the horse and against His army. And the beast was captured and with it the false prophet.... These two were thrown alive into the lake of fire that burns with sulfur. Rev. 19:20

You will make them [all Your enemies] like a fiery furnace when You appear. The Lord will swallow them up in His wrath, and fire will consume them. Ps. 21:9

The beast was slain and...thrown into the blazing fire. Dan. 7:11 NIV

For his burning place has long been prepared; ...the breath of the Lord, like a stream of sulphur, kindles it. Is. 30:33

And I turned you to ashes on the earth in the sight of all.... Ezek. 28:18b

When the thousand years are ended, satan will be released from his prison and will deceive the nations at the four corners of the earth...in order to gather them for battle; they are as numerous as the sands of the sea. They marched up over the breadth of the earth and surrounded the camp of the saints and the beloved city. And fire came down from heaven and consumed them. And the devil who had deceived them was thrown into the lake of fire and sulfur, where the beast and the false prophet were and they will be tormented day and night forever and ever. Rev. 20:7,10

The Dragon, Beast, and Death Destroyed (Cont.)

The last enemy to be destroyed is death. I Cor. 15:26

Then death and Hades were thrown into the Lake of Fire. Rev. 20:14

Then comes the end, when He [Jesus] hands over the kingdom to God the Father, after He has destroyed every ruler and every authority and power. I Cor. 15:24

Heaven and earth will pass away

"Heaven and earth will pass away, but My Words will not pass away." Matt. 24:35

"Heaven and earth will pass away, but My Words will not pass away." Mk. 13:31

"Heaven and earth will pass away, but My Words will not pass away." Lk. 21:35

The heavens will vanish like smoke, the earth will wear out like a garment. Is. 51:6

The earth shall be utterly laid waste and utterly despoiled; for the Lord has spoken this Word. The earth dries up and withers; the heavens languish together with the earth. Is. 24:3-4

They come from a distant land, from the end of the heavens, the Lord and the weapons of His indignation, to destroy the whole earth. Is. 13:5

I will utterly sweep away everything from the face of the earth, says the Lord.... On the day of the Lord's wrath; in the fire of His passion the whole earth shall be consumed; for a full, a terrible end He will make of all the inhabitants of the earth. Zeph. 1:1,18

The Lord of hosts, He who touches the earth and it melts and all who live in it mourn, ...the Lord is His Name. Amos 9:5,6

Then I saw a great white throne and the One sat on it; the earth and the heaven fled from His presence, and no place was found for them. Rev. 20:11

But by the same Word the present heavens and earth have been reserved for fire, being kept until the Day of Judgment and destruction of the godless. II Pet. 2:7

But the day of the Lord will come like a thief, and then the heavens will pass away with a loud noise, and the elements will be dissolved with fire, and the earth and everything that is done on it will be disclosed. [note: will be burned up] Since all these things are to be dissolved in this way, what sort of persons ought you to be in leading lives of holiness and Godliness, waiting for and hastening the coming of the day of God, because of which the heavens will be set ablaze and dissolved, and the elements will melt with fire? II Pet. 2:10-12

New Heaven and New Earth

But in accordance with His promise, we wait for new heavens and a new earth, where righteousness is at home. II Pet. 2:13

I am about to create new heavens and a new earth. Is. 65:17

For...the new heavens and the new earth, which I will make, shall remain before Me, says the Lord. Is. 66:22

Then I saw a new heaven and a new earth; for the first heaven and the first earth had passed away, and the sea was no more. Rev. 21:1

Jesus...must remain in heaven until the time of universal restoration that God announced long ago through His Holy prophets. Acts 4:21

New Heaven and New Earth (Cont.)

"At the **renewal of all things**, when the Son of Man is seated on the throne of His Glory, you who have followed Me will also sit on twelve thrones, judging the twelve tribes of Israel." Matt. 19:28

Come Quickly, Lord Jesus

And, behold, I come quickly; and My reward is with Me, to give every man according as his work shall be. Rev. 22:12 KJV

Behold I am coming quickly! Blessed is he who keeps the Words. Rev. 22:7 NKJV

He which testifieth these things saith, Surely I come quickly. Amen. Even so, come, Lord Jesus. Rev. 22:20 KJV

The Spirit and the bride say, "Come." And let everyone who hears say, "Come." Rev. 22:17 KJV

Our Lord, come! I Cor. 16:22

And the Lord whom you seek will suddenly come to His Temple. Mal. 3:1

So Christ...will appear a second time, not to deal with sin, but to save those who are eagerly waiting for Him. Heb. 9:28

Prayer for the Second Coming

Mar. 22, '06

O Yeshua, please come quickly! You spoke the Word that You would come soon and quickly. Please fulfill Your Word, Yeshua Adonai. Please come very soon! Your people need You to come soon!

O Yeshua, bring everything to pass that must come to pass—even the scary things, so You can come and take us home. O Yeshua, we stand with You against the enemy, we do warfare with You against him and all his hosts and his beasts and false prophets so they can all be banished from the earth. We speak to them in the mighty power of Your Holy Name to be removed from the earth and be cast into the Lake of Fire, to be gone forever and ever. Annihilate them with the breath of Your mouth so You can come and reign, Yeshua Adonai—You, our Lord and King and Redeemer and Bridegroom. May Your promises come to pass, Yeshua Adonai. Annihilate them with the breath of Your mouth, so You can come and reign.

Mar. 9, '06

...until the decreed end is poured out upon the desolator. Dan. 9:27

O Heavenly Father, You are the One who decides when the time is here. You are the One who commands the time of the end. You are the One who watches over Your Word to perform it (Jer. 1:12). Please pour out the decreed end upon the desolator. Please.

Mar. 24, '06

It is not for you to know the times or the seasons, which the Father hath put in His own power. Acts 1: 7 KJV

O Father, You are the One who holds the times and the seasons in Your hand. You are the One with the authority, who has set them. And You have given us access to Your throne through the Blood of Yeshua/Jesus, to bring petitions to You. O Father, I come with this petition: please bring Your decrees and Your times and Your seasons to fulfillment. Please make it be time, Heavenly Father. We have waited so long. Please don't make us wait any longer. PLEASE. Bring all Your prophecies to fulfillment. Let us come to the day when Your Glorious Kingdom, the Holy City, comes down out of Heaven—when there will no longer be any evil anywhere—when all will worship You and Glorify You. Bring it to pass, O Holy, Heavenly Father.

Nov. 18, '02

From *The Purpose Driven Life,* by Rick Warren, page 284: "We must remember that no matter how contented or successful people appear to be, without Christ they are hopelessly lost.... From page 286: "If you want Jesus to come back sooner, focus on fulfilling your mission...."

O Jesus I do want You to return. Help me to fulfill my mission. Give me an overflowing, overwhelming love for the lost! Send millions of workers to reach all the lost of the earth, so You can come to us to take all the redeemed home.

Oct. 27, '05

"I have trodden the wine press alone, and from the peoples no one was with Me; I trod them...in My wrath; their juice spattered...and stained all My robes." Is. 63:1-4

O Jesus, I'm so sorry You had to tread the wine press alone. I'm so sorry You had to get Your splendid robes stained. I'm sorry You had to have wrath for the people. I pray news of Your salvation will reach everyone, and that everyone will accept Your salvation and turn away from evil so You won't have to have wrath anymore.

It was...His presence that saved them. Is. 63:9

O Jesus bring Your presence to this earth to save it!! Bring Your mighty, powerful presence!! Your earth-shattering presence so all people will turn and receive Your redemption.

O that You would tear open the heavens and come down...that nations might tremble at Your presence. Is. 64:1,2

Yes, Jesus, COME!!

May 22, '02

I'm still praying for Jesus to come back. Reading James Dobson's letter is so discouraging. The U.S. and the world are just getting worse and worse.

There seems to be no hope, Jesus. Your coming back is the only hope for this world. We Christians are too human. It's time for You to return because while the Gospel is being preached to the whole world—while that is being accomplished— the original Christian country (U.S.) is becoming more and more heathen. O Lord Jesus, send revival again to America. Redeem it while the world is being redeemed, so You may come quickly and take us all to Yourself.

Nov. 23, '02

Everyone who has left houses...or children or fields, for My...sake... (Matt. 19:29). *Whoever comes to Me and does not hate...wife and children...yes, and even life itself, cannot be My disciple* (Lk. 14:26).

Everyone wants a nice home we all desire it. But instead of giving up that desire in order to spread the Gospel, we work hard and save until we can buy our dream place. Then we spend our whole lives taking care of it and paying for it.

Most of the whole world of Christians, now and over the centuries, have not put the mission of the Kingdom first. We've put marriage and family first; raising good kids first; and providing a nice life for our kids first. We've built a better world as far as conveniences go and we've spread democracy, but how about the Gospel? Some have given up all—houses and land and family—to spread the Gospel, but so few have. So few have fulfilled the Great commission. There's likely to be a lot of remorse about this at the judgment. Lots and lots. I'm feeling terrible regret right now for not doing my part.

O Jesus, forgive us. Perhaps You could've returned to earth sooner if we would've all given up everything to spread Your Word. Jesus, help young people today to see that they can give up houses and land, spouses and children before they have them, so they can be free to carry out Your Great Commission.

Mar. 25, '06

Why don't we focus better on the Great Commission? I'm thinking today that it is because we are like the servant who hid his talent (Matt. 25:14-30). God gave the servants money, but only as a loan. They not only had to give it all back but also all the increase they worked hard to make from it. The first two gave it all back with no resentment for their unpaid hard work. They were happy to do it! The third guy didn't want to work hard like that if he didn't get to keep any of it for himself. He didn't want to spend his own energy and sweat totally for another man's gain and none of his own.

Well, that's the way most of us are!! —Especially toward God! Most of us are spending our lives doing things for ourselves—to have a better house, a better car, good children, a good future, honor, respect, financial security, a good retirement, nice vacations, and on and on and on. We aren't doing it to give it all back to God or to just benefit and spread the Kingdom! The first two men worked hard and smart only for God's benefit.

O Lord, change our hearts and minds until we see how astronomically more important Your Kingdom work is than absolutely anything else! Help us to work hard for You instead of for ourselves so the Gospel will reach the ends of the earth (Matt. 24:14) and You can come again to receive us unto Yourself (Jn. 14:3 KJV).

Dec. 4, '02

O Jesus, please come back soon and bathe the whole world in Your Love.

Dec. 31, '03

Come, Lord Jesus. Please return to earth and take Your Bride Home.

April 28, '04

Is Your coming near? Come Lord Jesus, COME QUICKLY!! Your Bride is waiting for you.

Dec. 22, '05

Come, Lord Jesus, come quickly Your people in all the world, Your Bride from all the nations, is waiting for You!

1999 or so

Jesus, are You waiting for Your people to long for You with one heart and one soul before You come? Help us to be united in crying out for You to return. Maybe You are waiting for our worship songs to be begging You to return. Let that come to pass. Let the whole world over be singing songs of longing and pleading for Your return to take us home. Place that longing in Your people, Jesus.

Mar. 23, '06

O Yeshua, put it on people's hearts to pray for Your return. Call intercessors to pray for the preparation for Your return. Call many modern John the Baptists for today who will "prepare the way" for You. Call Anna's and Simeon's to spend their time praying for Your second appearing like the first Anna and Simeon prayed for Your first coming. Lord, I ask for an army of people to be doing prayer warfare for all things to be accomplished so You can soon return. Come, Lord Jesus/Yeshua Adonai. We are pining for You like a Bride pining for her Bridegroom.

It is your Father's good pleasure to give you the Kingdom. Luke 12:32

The Beauty
After The End

Be comforted as you pray these
marvelous prophecies into existence.

The whole earth is at rest and quiet; they break forth into singing. Is. 14:7

The wilderness and the dry land shall be glad, the desert shall rejoice and blossom [as a rose (KJV)]; like the crocus it shall blossom abundantly, and rejoice with joy and singing.... They shall see the Glory of the Lord, the Majesty of our God.... For waters shall break forth in the wilderness and streams in the desert. A highway shall be there and it shall be called the Holy Way; the unclean shall not travel on it, but it shall be for God's people; no traveler, not even fools shall go astray....the redeemed shall walk there. And the ransomed of the Lord shall return, and come to Zion with singing; everlasting joy shall be upon their heads; they shall obtain joy and gladness, and sorrow and sighing shall flee away. Is. 35:1-2,6,8-10

Therefore the redeemed of the Lord shall return, and come with singing unto Zion; and everlasting joy shall be upon their head: they shall obtain gladness and joy; and sorrow and mourning shall flee away. I, even I, am He that comforteth you. Is. 51:11 KJV

In the days to come the mountain of the Lord's house shall be established as the highest of the mountains, and shall be raised above the hills; all the nations shall stream to it. Many people shall come and say, "Come, let us go up to the mountain of the Lord, to the house of the God of Jacob; that He may teach us His ways and that we may walk in His paths. Is. 2:1-4 and Micah 4:1-4 (These two passages are exactly the same!)

On that day the deaf shall hear the Words of a scroll, and out of their gloom and darkness the eyes of the blind shall see. The meek shall obtain fresh joy in the Lord, and the neediest people shall exult in the Holy One of Israel. For the tyrant shall be no more, and the scoffer shall cease to be. Is. 29:18-20

They shall beat their swords into plowshares, and their spears into pruning hooks; Nation shall not lift up sword against nation, neither shall they learn war any more. Is. 2:4

No longer shall they teach one another, or say to each other, "know the Lord," for they shall all know Me, from the least of them to the greatest, says the Lord. Jer. 31:33-34

All shall know Me from the least of them to the greatest. Heb. 8:11

Sing, O heavens, for the Lord has done it; shout, O depths of the earth; break forth into singing, O mountains, O forest, and every tree in it! For the Lord has redeemed.

Is. 44:23

Arise, shine, for your light has come, and the Glory of the Lord has risen upon you... The Lord will arise upon you and His Glory will appear over you. Nations shall come to your light, and kings to the brightness of your dawn..... Then you shall see and be radiant; your heart shall thrill and rejoice. Is. 60:1-3,5

Be glad and rejoice forever in what I am creating; for I am about to create Jerusalem as a joy, and its people as a delight. Is. 65:18

Then I saw the holy city, the New Jerusalem, coming down out of heaven from God.

Rev. 21:2

I will rejoice in Jerusalem, and delight in My people; no more shall the sound of weeping be heard...or the cry of distress. No more shall there be an infant that lives but a few days, or an old person who does not live out a lifetime. Is. 65:19-20

And no inhabitant will say, "I am sick." Is. 33:24

Death will be no more; mourning and crying and pain will be no more, for the first things have passed away. Rev. 21:4

The wolf and the lamb shall feed together, the lion shall eat straw like the ox; but the serpent—its food shall be dust! They shall no longer hurt or destroy.... Is. 65:25

See, the home of God is among mortals. He will dwell with them as their God.... He will wipe every tear from their eyes. Rev. 21:3

Then the Lord my God will come, and all the holy ones with Him. On that day there shall not be either cold or frost. And there shall be continuous day…for at evening time there shall be light. On that day living waters shall flow.... And the Lord will become King over all the earth. Zech. 14:5-7,8,9

The sun shall no longer be your light by day, nor for brightness shall the moon give light to you by night; but the Lord will be your everlasting light, and your God will be your glory. Your sun shall no more go down, or your moon withdraw itself; for the Lord will be your everlasting light. Is. 60:19-20

And I saw no temple in the city, for its temple is the Lord God the Almighty and the Lamb. And the city has no need of sun or moon to shine on it, for the Glory of God is its light, and its lamp is the Lamb. The nations will walk by its light, and the kings of the earth will bring their glory into it. Its gates will never be shut by day—and there will be no night there. People will bring into it the glory and the honor of the nations. But nothing unclean will enter it.
Rev. 21:22-27

The treasure of all nations shall come, and I will fill this house with splendor, says the Lord of hosts. Haggai 2:7

Then the angel showed me the River of the Water of Life, bright as crystal, flowing from the throne.... On either side of the River is the Tree of Life…and the leaves of the Tree are for the healing of the nations. Rev. 22:1-2

Nothing accursed will be found there any more. But the throne of God and of the Lamb will be in it, and His servants will worship Him; they will see His face, and His Name will be on their foreheads. And there will be no more night; they need no light of lamp or sun, for the Lord God will be their Light, and they will reign forever and ever. Rev. 22:3-5

Prayer

O Yeshua, these Scriptures are so beautiful—soooooo awesomely beautiful. Yeshua, bring the day when this, too, shall come to pass. O how we long to be in the city where the only Light is the Light of Your Glorious presence. We long to be with You, Yeshua, and behold Your Heavenly Face, and soak in Your Love.

O Master, help us to reach the ends of the earth with Your Gospel, and to disciple the nations so these Scriptures of splendor can be fulfilled. And O, Savior, Lord and King, show us how to keep on warring with You to conquer and banish evil from the universe so You may return and receive us into this astonishingly, marvelous Holy City.

I...meditate on You. Psalms 63:6

The Glorious Greatness
of Our Lord

Let's finish by meditating again on our Glorious God. May we be astounded at His awesomeness.

"Worthy is the Lamb that was slaughtered to receive Power and Wealth and Wisdom and Might and Honor and Glory and Blessing...forever and ever.... Amen!" Rev. 5:11,13

"You are worthy...for You were slaughtered and by Your Blood You ransomed for God saints from every tribe and language and people and nation. You have made them to be a kingdom [KJV: kings] and priests serving our God...forever and ever." Rev. 5:9-10,13

"Holy, Holy, Holy...Lord God Almighty who was and is and is to come." ...[G]ive Glory and Honor and thanks to the One seated on the throne who lives forever and ever.... "You are worthy our Lord and God to receive Glory and Honor and Power for You created all things and by Your will they existed and were created." Rev. 4:8,9,11

"Worship Him who made heaven and earth, the sea and the springs of water." Rev. 14:7

"You are the Lord...alone; You have made heaven, the heaven of heavens with all their host, the earth and all that is on it, the seas and all that is in them. To all of them You give life, and the host of heaven worships You." Neh. 9:6

"Rejoice...you heavens and those who dwell in them." Rev. 12:12

"Let us rejoice and exult and give Him the Glory." Rev. 19:7

"Blessing and Glory and Wisdom and Thanksgiving and Honor and Power and Might be to [You] our God forever and ever! Amen." Rev. 7:12

There is no one like You, O Lord, and there is no God besides You. I Chron. 17:20

There is none like You...O Lord, nor are there any works like Yours. Ps. 86:8

"Great and amazing are Your deeds Lord God Almighty. Just and True are Your ways, King of the nations! [note: King of the Ages]. [O] Lord, who will not fear and Glorify Your Name? For You alone are Holy." Rev. 15:3-4

Sing to the Lord a new song for He has done marvelous things. His right hand and His Holy arm have gotten Him victory.... He has revealed...[His righteousness (KJV)] in the sight of the nations.... All the ends of the earth have seen the victory [KJV: the salvation] of our God. Ps. 98:1-3

O the depth of [Your] riches and [Your] wisdom and [Your] knowledge [O] God! How unsearchable are [Your] judgments and how inscrutable [Your] ways! ... For from [You] and through [You] and to [You] are all things. To [You] be the Glory forever. Amen. Rom. 11:33,36

"We give thanks [to You], Lord God Almighty, who are and were for You have taken Your Great Power and begun to reign." Rev. 11:17

You have exalted Your Word and Your Name above everything. Ps. 138:26

The whole earth is full of [Your] Glory. Is. 6:3

"Hallelujah for the Lord our God the Almighty reigns." Rev. 19:6

"The kingdom of the world has become the Kingdom of [You] our Lord and of [You our] Messiah and [You] will reign forever and ever." Rev. 11:15

"Behold, heaven and the [highest (NRSV)] heaven of heavens cannot contain You."
I Kings 8:27 NKJV

"O Lord, You have only begun to show...Your Greatness and Your Might."
Deut. 3:23

Prayer

Yes, Lord! You have only barely begun to show Yourself!! Show us more, Lord! Prepare the world to be able to see. Prepare me. Let the day come when You don't have to hold back anymore—when You can show Your FULL GLORY!!

FOREVER AND EVER!! HALLELUJAH!! AMEN!

And they [who conquered the enemy] loved not their lives. (KJV)

They did not cling to life even in the face of death. (NRSV)

Revelations 12:11